My Seal on His Heart

Eucharistic Intimacy in the Song of Songs

Gregory Cleveland, OMV

En Route Books and Media, LLC
Saint Louis, MO

ENROUTE
Make the time

En Route Books and Media, 5705 Rhodes Avenue, St. Louis, MO 63109

Contact us at
contactus@enroutebooksandmedia.com

ISBN-13: 979-8-88870-505-6
Library of Congress Control Number: 2026934672

Nihil Obstat granted by Fr. Jim Walther, OMV
Superior of the St. Ignatius Province of the Oblates of the Virgin Mary

Table of Contents

Table of Contents

Introduction

The marriage metaphor for God's union with his people is found throughout the Old Testament, for example in Hosea (chaps. 1–3), Ezekiel (chap. 16), Jeremiah (chap. 2), and the entire Song of Songs. From ancient times the Song of Songs has been understood in religious terms as an expression of the covenantal love between God and the Jewish people. It is interesting then that the Jews read the Song of Songs throughout the eight days of Passover. In so doing, they recast the entire Exodus story of Israel's liberation from slavery in Egypt in terms of a love story wherein the Lord chose them as his people for marriage. The Song of Songs is therefore a fervent and poetic expression of God's love for Israel, and her love for God in return. Rabbi Akiva's declaration highlights its significance in Jewish tradition: "Nothing in the entire world is worthy but for that day on which the Song of Songs was given to Israel. For all the Scriptures are holy, but the Song of Songs is the Holy of Holies!"[1] The Zohar, Judaism's most mystical text, asserts that the Song of Songs embodies the entire Torah, which further underscores its mystical and spiritual importance.

[1] Mishnah Yadavim 3:5.

The Holy Eucharist is the fulfillment of the Passover meal and celebrates the new Exodus that Jesus makes by his passion, death, and resurrection. In this new Exodus, we are liberated from slavery to sin and led through the desert of this life to the promised land of eternal life. Jesus' love story is more personal, more passionate, and more sacrificial than what was prefigured in the Old Testament. In this New Passover, Jesus expresses his desire to live in us as we live in him, laying down his life on the Cross to redeem and espouse us. How much more ought we to read the Song of Songs at the New Passover of the Eucharist to fathom the depths of Christ's love for us? Jesus fulfills what was foretold of the Messiah-Bridegroom in the Song of Songs as a lover who takes his bride, the Church, to himself in marriage.

Jesus is the Bridegroom (cf. Mk 2:19; Mt 9:15; Jn 3:29) and the Church is his bride (cf. Eph 5:25-27). The Lord's Supper is the wedding banquet (cf. Rv 19:9) in which Jesus gives himself entirely to his bride in a new and everlasting marriage covenant. Pope St. John Paul II frequently spoke of the nuptial character of the Eucharist, "The Eucharist is the sacrament of our redemption. It is the sacrament of the Bridegroom and of the Bride."[2] Moreover, "the entire Christian life

---

[2] St. John Paul II, Apostolic Letter *Mulieris Dignitatem*, 26. (Vatican City, Libreria Editrice Vaticana, 1988). Online at https://www.vatican.va/content/john-paul-ii/en/apost_letters/

bears the mark of the spousal love of Christ and the Church. Already Baptism, the entry into the People of God, is a nuptial mystery; it is so to speak the nuptial bath which precedes the wedding feast, the Eucharist."[3]

The Holy Eucharist is truly a banquet in which the Lord gives his very self as our food and drink. The bride of the Song is brought to the banqueting house by her Beloved and is fed and nourished by his love. "His intention toward me was love" (Sg 2:4). The early Christians referred to the Eucharist as the *Agape* or "Love Feast" (cf. Jude 12). St. Thomas Aquinas called the Eucharist the sacrament of love or "charity." Love seeks either to possess what is loved or to bestow benefit upon it, seeking to be united with its beloved.[4] Jesus desires to be one with us just as he and the Father are one. "As the Father has loved me, so I have loved you; abide in my love" (Jn 15:9).

We could explain love as the gift of oneself to another person. Jesus' spousal love for the Church is best expressed through the Eucharist. Jesus not only declares his love for the

---

1988/documents/hf_jp-ii_apl_19880815_mulieris-dignitatem.html

[3] Benedict XVI, *Sacramentum Caritatis*, 27 (Vatican City, Libreria Editrice Vaticana, 2007). Online at https://www.vatican.va/content/benedict-xvi/en/apost_exhortations/documents/hf_ben-xvi_exh_20070222_sacramentum-caritatis.html

[4] See *ST* I-IIae, Q. 28.

Church in the Eucharist, but he also demonstrates this love by genuinely offering himself to her as the divine Bridegroom, both in body and in spirit. In his writings, Pope Benedict XVI characterizes the Eucharist as the ultimate manifestation of the sacrificial love that Jesus revealed on the cross.

In the Eucharist Jesus not only tells the Church he loves her; he shows his love by really and truly giving himself to her, in both body and spirit, as the divine Bridegroom. Benedict describes the Eucharist as the premier expression of the sacrificial love that Jesus demonstrated on the cross when he writes:

> The Eucharist draws us into Jesus' act of self-oblation. More than just statically receiving the incarnate Logos, we enter the very dynamic of his self-giving. The imagery of marriage between God and Israel is now realized in a way previously inconceivable: it had meant standing in God's presence, but now it becomes union with God through sharing in Jesus' self-gift, sharing in his body and blood.... We can thus understand how *agape* also became a term for the Eu-

> charist: there God's own agape comes to us bodily, in order to continue his work in us and through us.[5]

Because it enables us to intimately experience our Lord's Passion and truly absorb him into ourselves, the Eucharist is also known as the sacrament of love. By making a commitment to this unity with Christ, who is here with us, we can partake in the joy of paradise, where we will be united with God in glory.

Just as the Hebrews read the Song of Songs at Passover, we can interpret the New Passover, the holy Eucharist, as Jesus' wedding banquet of love and sacrifice. Through our devotion and fervent reception of the Sacrament of his passion and love, may we always experience the goodness of the Risen Lord as we continue to conform ourselves to Him, who is our salvation and our hope.

---

[5] Benedict XVI, *Deus Caritas Est*, 13–14. (Vatican City, Libreria Editrice Vaticana, 2005). Online at https://www.vatican.va/content/benedict-xvi/en/encyclicals/documents/hf_ben-xvi_enc_20051225_deus-caritas-est.html

1

Invitation

"Alleluia! For the Lord our God the Almighty reigns.
Let us rejoice and exult and give him the glory,
for the marriage of the Lamb has come,
and his Bride has made herself ready (Rv 19:7).

The Spirit and the Bride say, "Come." And let him who hears say, "Come." And let him who is thirsty come, let him who desires take the water of life without price (Rv 22:17).

Draw me after you, let us make haste.
The king has brought me into his chambers. (Sg 1:4)

As a newly ordained priest, I performed twelve weddings in my first three months, spending a great deal of time preparing each couple for perhaps the biggest day of their lives. I felt chills run down my spine when the bride appeared in all her glory to walk down the aisle. I would often whisper words of encouragement to the groom who appeared overwhelmed with the realization of what he was doing—laying down his life for his bride. Jesus would sustain them sacramentally, not only as the goal of their marriage, but as its animating principle of love. I as a priest and the entire congregation as the Body of Christ, were there to support and encourage the bride and groom in their holy endeavor. Our joy was palpable in our hearts and throughout the Church.

The Honor of Your Presence is Requested

Imagine receiving a wedding invitation from a great king. Think of the honor of attending. This dream comes true every week when we celebrate the Sunday Eucharist. Jesus Christ, the king, takes the Church, his bride in marriage. Saint Augustine writes that every Eucharistic celebration is a renewal of the wedding of Christ and the Church:

> Every Celebration of the Eucharist is a celebration of Marriage; the Church's nuptials are celebrated. The King's Son is about to marry a wife, and the King's Son is himself a King; and the guests frequenting the marriage are themselves the Bride.... For all the Church is Christ's Bride, of which the beginning and first-fruits is the Flesh of Christ, because there was the Bride joined to the Bridegroom in the flesh.[6]

---

[6] St. Augustine, *Homily 2 on 1 John*. PL 35. Online at https://www.newadvent.org/fathers/170202.htm

Christ marries not just the Church collectively as a whole, but each of us individually. Each of us is the spouse of Christ united with him in his body and blood. Just as the two become one in marriage, we become one body and one spirit in Christ in the deepest possible union. While human marriage pales in comparison to the degree of union we experience with the Lord in Holy Communion, it is still the best analogy to describe the union. Christ lays down his life for us on the cross and gives us his flesh and blood to eat and drink. He invites us to live in him as he lives in us. Every Mass is the consummation of our marriage vows with the Lord, whereby he pledges himself to us and we offer ourselves to him in return. Married couples ought to frequently renew their commitment to their marriage partner, and so should we often do so with Christ our spouse.

At the end of the book of Revelation, the final book of the Bible, we receive a wedding invitation to "the marriage of the Lamb." (Rv 19:7). The Lamb is Jesus Christ, who was slain on the Cross but is now triumphant in heaven, seated on the altar. Two figures, the Holy Spirit and the bride (the Church) issue this invitation, saying "Come!" The Church is revealed as the bride adorned for her husband and as the holy city, the new Jerusalem, coming down from heaven (Rv 21:2). As members of the Church, each of us is the spouse of Christ. The Holy Spirit prompts us to be joined as the Body of Christ, the Church, and to experience this wedding feast in the Holy Eucharist, a foretaste of heavenly beatitude.

Welcomed and Encouraged

The Spirit gathers us for every Eucharist. As members of his body we are one in him and see Christ in one another. When the congregation gathers in his name, Christ is present, as he promised us "For where two or three are gathered in my name, there am I in the midst of them" (Mt 18:20). *The Didache*, also known as the "Teaching of the Twelve Apostles," is an ancient Christian text that provides instructions on various aspects of Christian life. One of its passages beautifully illustrates the symbolism of unity within the Church using the metaphor of bread made from many grains: "As this broken bread was once scattered on the mountains, and after it had been brought together became one, so may your Church be gathered together from the ends of the earth into your kingdom."[7]

Just as the scattered grains of wheat come together to form a single loaf of bread, so too should the varied members of the Church unite as one body, bound together by our faith

---

[7] The Didache 9:4, trans. Charles H. Hoole, St. Pachomius Orthodox Library, October/November 1994, The Didache (uoregon.edu). Online at https://pages.uoregon.edu/sshoemak/321/texts/didache.html

in Christ. The Eucharist, which is the body and blood of Christ, serves as a powerful symbol of this unity. St. Cyprian, a third century bishop, echoed this concept, stating that the bread and wine in the Eucharist symbolizes the unity of Christians, strengthened by indivisible charity: "The sacrifices of the Lord themselves highlight the unanimity of Christians strengthened by solid, indivisible charity. For when the Lord calls the bread formed of the union of many grains his body, and when he calls the wine pressed from many clusters of grapes and poured together his blood, in the same way he indicates our flock formed of a multitude united together."[8]

Friends You Haven't Met Yet

We are already one as members of the Body of Christ. "Now you are the body of Christ and individually members of it" (1 Cor 12:27). This should make us intent on fellowship with one another as we gather. When we meet others in the parking lot and as we enter the foyer of the church we ought to greet each other warmly and kindly and even introduce

---

[8] St. Cyprian of Carthage, *Ep. ad Magnum,* 6, in St. John Paul II, General Audience, November 8, 2000 (Vatican City, Libreria Editrice Vaticana, 2000), 8 November 2000. Online at https://www.vatican.va/content/john-paul-ii/en/audiences/2000/documents/hf_jp-ii_aud_20001108.html

ourselves to others we don't yet know. The greeters or ushers are often tasked with this, but we can all participate in welcoming one another. No one should feel ignored or isolated as brothers and sisters in Christ. Our awareness of Christ's presence in the members of the congregation raises our respect for one another in attending the Eucharist.

The Eucharist is the culmination of God's action sanctifying the world in Christ and of the worship men and women offer to Christ and through him to the Father in the Holy Spirit. It is the efficacious sign and sublime cause of that communion in the divine life and that unity of the People of God by which the Church is kept in being.[9] Because the Eucharist renews the same gift that unites us as the Church, its communal aspect is central to its meaning. The Church community as a whole and not just a large number of people, is who receives the Eucharist. As the Eucharist renews our relationship as brothers and sisters, taking care of one another and cooperating to offer testimony to the united life of the Kingdom of God, we should always be aware of those with whom we receive. Our union with one another deepens as

---

[9] See Vatican II, *Constitution on the Liturgy, Sacrosanctum Concilium*, 10. (Vatican City, Libreria Editrice Vaticana, 1964). Online at https://www.vatican.va/archive/hist_councils/ii_vatican_council/documents/vat-ii_const_19631204_sacrosanctum-concilium_en.html

we worship the Lord together. In the words of theologian Romano Guardini:

> Congregation is formed only when those individuals are present not only corporeally, but also spiritually, when they have contacted one another in prayer and step together into the spiritual 'space' around them; strictly speaking, when they have first widened and heightened that space by prayer. Then true congregation comes into being, which, along with the building that is its architectural expression, forms the vital church in which the sacred act is accomplished.[10]

Where You Belong

The Lord made a covenant with Israel and with all those who made up the people. It was not with individual Hebrews one by one. Individuals were covenanted because they belonged to a covenanted community. There was a radically social sense of individual reality and no private covenants with Yahweh. In Christ, communion with God becomes a more sublime reality. Jesus gives human beings a share in His divine nature. The sharing in the Eucharistic body of Christ

---

[10] Romano Guardini, *Meditations before Mass* (Bloomington, IN, Indiana University Press, 1939). Online at https://guardini.wordpress.com/meditations-before-mass/

brings about at one and the same time communion with the Son. "The cup of blessing that we bless, is it not a participation in the blood of Christ? The bread that we break, is it not a participation in the body of Christ?" (1 Cor 10:16) Our fellowship with Jesus brings about the union of the members of his Body. "Because the loaf of bread is one, we, though many, are one body, for we all partake of the one loaf" (1 Cor 10:17).

The gift of the Holy Spirit to all Christians sets the seal on the intimate communion between us. The fraternal union of the first Christians is the result of our common faith in the Lord Jesus, of our desire to imitate Him together and of our love for him, from which our mutual love is born. "The community of believers was of one heart and mind, and no one claimed that any of his possessions was his own, but they had everything in common. With great power the apostles bore witness to the resurrection of the Lord Jesus, and great favor was accorded them all" (Acts 4:32-37). This communion between them is realized in the first place in the breaking of bread: "And they devoted themselves to the apostles' teaching and fellowship, to the breaking of bread and the prayers" (Acts 2:42).

The Eucharist is both the symbol and cause of communal unity. According to Luigi Guissani, belonging is the ultimate standard for embracing all reality:

> We are made by a belonging—belonging is more original to us than our solitude. If there weren't the awareness of a belonging, then the human being would be faced with his own nothingness. To be myself I need someone else. Alone, we cannot be ourselves. Christ is realized in us and among us through our companionship. That for which the 'I' is made and for which it does everything is a Presence.[11]

As the Body of Christ, we really do belong to one another in the Church. The Spirit and the Bride say "Come," join this communion in the Body of Christ.

- *Reflect* on the great honor of being invited to the King's wedding, and even greater esteem of being chosen as a spouse for marriage.
- *Ponder* the feeling of being united with your brothers and sisters in faith as you gather with them for the Holy Eucharist. How do you experience the Eucharist making you one in communion with God and one another?
- *Pray* with Rv 19:7 and 22:17. As you think about attending Mass this coming Sunday, ponder the invita-

[11] Luigi Giussani, *Generating Traces in the World: Acts of the International Meeting of the Ecclesial Movements, Rimini, 30 May-1 June 1997* (Milan: Editrice La Scuola, 1997), 131.

tion of the Spirit and the Bride to "Come!" Consider whose wedding feast it is, Christ our King, the Lamb of God who was slain and rose again, and how the bride makes herself ready.

2

Preparation

O that he would kiss me with the kisses of his mouth!
For your love is better than wine,
Draw me after you, let us make haste.
The king has brought me into his chambers. (Sg 1:2, 4a)

Love begins with desiring the beloved. The bride, Israel, desires the presence and kiss of the Bridegroom, the Lord. The kiss is an expression and experience of the bond of love between two people. A kiss unleashes feelings of attachment, affection, and devotion. At the physical level, the facial nerve carries messages to the brain that generate hormones, neurotransmitters, and natural endorphins, which rush through the body to produce the euphoria most people feel during a good kiss. Therefore, a kiss is a wonderful metaphor for describing the experience of God's love on a spiritual level, which may involve certain psychological, emotional, and even physical manifestations. Who wouldn't want to be kissed by God? According to St. Bernard and a long mystical tradition in the Church, the kiss desired by the bride is God's kiss of the Holy Spirit.

The bride is *ready* to be kissed. This presumes that the relationship has reached a certain stage of development where she trusts her lover. Some people may not have spent enough time seeking a real relationship with God to even ask or desire such a kiss. Prayer is the forging of that relationship with God. The Latin word for prayer, *oration*, means the mouth and the lips and is the basis for this kiss of God. The sacraments are intensified moments of intimacy and bonding with our Lord. In Holy Communion we kiss God, as it were, when we receive him in the Eucharist. God is passing his supernatural food and life on to us with his kiss in the Mass. In this marvelous exchange, God is transferring his divine Spirit to us, and we are transferring our human spirit to Him.

Incarnation, the Holy Spirit, and Union

The bride now expresses intense desire for the kiss of her bridegroom. As a figure of Israel, we can imagine her heightened longing for the coming of the Messiah, and the great anticipation of his near arrival. The kiss of God happened with the coming of Christ in the Incarnation, when the divine and human touched and united. As the Word of God, we can imagine Jesus as the mouth of the Father and his breath in speaking symbolized by the Holy Spirit. Word and breath always go together, as do the Son and the Spirit. Jesus kisses forth the Spirit as the revelation and mouth of the Father. The Father and the Son breathe the Spirit forth in their eternal love as the kiss of God to us. The kiss is the Holy Spirit, God's gift of his very self to us.

St. Ambrose specifically linked the act of approaching the altar to the words of the Song of Songs 1:1, interpreting the "kiss" as a mystical union between Christ and the soul. In his work *On the Sacraments* Ambrose addresses the newly baptized Christians, explaining the profound meaning behind the liturgical actions they have just experienced. He states: "You have come to the altar, the Lord Jesus calls you, for the text speaks of you or of the Church, and he says to you: 'Let him kiss me with kisses of his mouth'" (Sg 1:1). Ambrose uses this verse to explain the worthiness and intimacy of receiving the heavenly sacraments. He notes the verse can be applied to Christ, who, seeing the soul pure from sin, judges it worthy of the sacraments and invites it to the heavenly banquet with a kiss. He also encourages the individual to apply it to oneself, seeing oneself as worthy to approach the altar of Christ and saying, "May he kiss me with the kiss of his mouth," which is a desire for a kiss from Christ. For Ambrose, the physical actions in the liturgy, the priest kissing the altar and the faithful approaching the altar to receive the Eucharist, are the fulfillment of this intimate, spiritual embrace described in the Song of Songs. They symbolize the deep love, forgiveness, and a profound, personal union with Christ. He also taught that the altar itself is an "image of the Body of Christ."[12]

Prayer Is the Prelude

Like the bride, we are longing for that kiss of God and preparing to receive it. Jesus prepares us to receive him by sending his Holy Spirit to us, to help us long for his presence. The lyrics of Duke Ellington's *Prelude to a Kiss* speak to us of our heart's desire for the only one who can satisfy our longings. We could imagine singing this song to the Lord, or the Lord, in his true humanity, singing it to us.

Oh, how my love song gently cries
For the tenderness within your eyes
My love is a prelude that never dies
A prelude to a kiss[13]

From the depths of our souls we are longing for the Lord's tender presence. Like a lover serenading his beloved, he gains our attention and speaks to our hearts. His presence and touch transform us. Repeatedly, we experience this longing

---

[12] St. Ambrose, *De Sacramentis* IV. 7 (PL 16, 447). Online at https://www.newadvent.org/fathers/3405.htm

[13] *Prelude to a Kiss*, words and music by Duke Ellington, Irving Mills and Irving Gordon, 1938.

and fulfillment and will do so for all eternity in his love which never dies.

Preparation for holy Mass is our prelude to a kiss. Our best preparation is to maintain a constant life of prayer in our daily lives. Prayer will create the fertile soil in which the seed of Christ's Word and Body can be sown. We pray each day during the week and especially before Mass. According to the Archbishop of Milan, Carlo Martini:

> All of this (making the Eucharist a way of life) requires, in practice, that we develop interior attitudes that precede, accompany, and follow the Eucharistic celebration: listening to the revealed word, contemplation of the mysteries of Jesus, confrontation between the way of life that springs from the paschal and Eucharistic mystery and the ever-new spiritual situations in which the community and single believers find themselves. In this, silent prayer, listening to the Word of God, meditation of Scripture, and personal reflection are not separate from the Eucharist but vitally connected to it. [14]

---

[14] C. M. Martini, Pastoral Letter, *The Contemplative Dimension of Life, Letter to the Clergy and Faithful of the Ambrosian Archdiocese for the pastoral year 1980-81* (Milan, 1980).

Prayer will keep us in tune with the Holy Spirit and a sense of wonder toward the Holy Eucharist. The person who wonders is responsive to reality and appreciative of the richness, depth, mystery, and beauty of being. The wondering person searches for the springs of reality; the why, the how, the how-much-more. This person is fascinated and joyful, alive, physically and intellectually. The wonderer is struck by what he has seen and tasted, sensitive to the inexhaustible depth of the smallest realities. Wonder is the experience and living of a marvel. He or she must wonder not only at the reality, but at the fountain of reality, the source. One is aware that much more lies beyond his vision and he is fascinated. St. John Paul II explains:

> For those who know how to read deeply, each thing, each event carries a message that, in the final analysis, leads to God. The revealing sings of God's presence, therefore, are multiple. But in order not to miss them, we must be pure and simple, like children, capable of admiring, being astonished, of marveling, and being enchanted by the divine gestures of love and closeness we witness.[15]

---

[15] Pope St. John Paul II, Homily in Lyon (October 7, 1986). Online at https://www.vatican.va/content/john-paul-ii/it/homilies/1986/documents/hf_jp-ii_hom_19861007_annency-francia.html

As one searches the mystery, one finds meaning, and meaning opens to greater mysteries. This is how we should approach the Mass, with wonder.

Rekindling Wonder and Awe

Pope St. John Paul II invited Catholics to regain a sense of "Eucharistic amazement." When we celebrate the Eucharist, we can relive, in some way, the experience of the two disciples on the road to Emmaus. Just as their eyes were opened, and they recognized Jesus (Lk 24:31), our encounter with the Eucharist should evoke a similar sense of wonder and recognition. Amazement is our immediate response to the reality of Christ's true presence as a friend who fulfills our deepest desires.[16]

The Italian youth St. Carlo Acutis, who died in 2006, was well known for his intense devotion to the Eucharist and demonstrated Eucharistic amazement throughout his life. He spent much time in Eucharistic adoration and referred to the Eucharist as his "highway to heaven." He explained that when

[16] See Pope St. John Paul II. *Ecclesia de Eucharistia*, 5, 6 (2003) and *Mane nobiscum Domine* (2004). Online at https://www.vatican.va/content/john-paul-ii/en/encyclicals/documents/hf_jp-ii_enc_20030417_eccl-de-euch.html and https://www.vatican.va/content/john-paul-ii/en/apost_letters/2004/documents/hf_jp-ii_apl_20041008_mane-nobiscum-domine.html

we face the sun we become tan, but when we place ourselves in front of the Eucharistic Jesus, we become saints. Carlo was so devoted to the Eucharist that he built a website to compile and disseminate information about Eucharistic miracles around the globe. Carlo was a young man, yet his faith had a profound effect on everyone around him. He encouraged his loved ones and friends to regularly attend Mass and partake in Communion. He is a role model for many, particularly young people, because of his commitment to the Eucharist and his use of technology to promote this devotion.

St. Carlo prepared for daily Mass with great care and dedication, receiving the Eucharist as often as possible. Here are some of the ways he prepared:

- Holy Hours: He made Holy Hours before or after Mass, spending time in adoration of the Blessed Sacrament.
- Confession: Carlo went to confession weekly to stay spiritually prepared.
- Rosary and Prayer: He prayed the Rosary daily and had a deep devotion to the Blessed Virgin Mary.
- Scripture Reading: Carlo meditated on passages from sacred Scripture regularly.
- Visits to the Tabernacle: He made visits to Jesus in the tabernacle each day.

Carlo's preparation for Mass was a testament to his deep faith and love for the Eucharist.

- *Reflect* on your own preparation for Mass. Do any of Carlo Acutis' practices resonate with you? What difference does contemplative prayer with Sacred Scripture make for you? In what ways do you experience Eucharistic amazement?
- *Pray* with Sg 1:2-4 and the bride's desire for the kiss of her lover. Consider your experience of the Lord's kiss of the Holy Spirit in the holy Eucharist.

3

Entrance Procession

Draw me after you, let us make haste.
The king has brought me into his chambers. (Sg 1:4)

The Mass is an Epiphany—a wondrous manifestation of God's glory as the Word made flesh—once in history at Bethlehem, and now in mystery in the Holy Eucharist. Pope Benedict XVI called the journey of the Magi toward the Epiphany at Bethlehem, "just the beginning of a great procession that continues throughout history. With the Magi, humanity's pilgrimage to Jesus Christ begins."[17] The amazing star that shines in the sky and calls out to the three wise men to follow signals the start of the Epiphany event. They perceive a glimmer of hope, a brilliant promise, and a new horizon to seek in its light. One of the first things we notice in the church when we arrive for Mass is that the candles on the altar and the vigil light by the tabernacle are lit. Like the Star of Beth-

[17] Benedict XVI, *Homily*, 6 January 2012: Solemnity of the Epiphany of the Lord, Vatican City, Libreria Editrice Vaticana. Online at https://www.vatican.va/content/benedict-xvi/en/homilies/2012/documents/hf_ben-xvi_hom_20120106_epifania.html

lehem, the lit candles suggest something holy that will happen in the sanctuary shortly. They herald the wonder that is about to happen here: heaven and earth coming together in the Sacrament of the Altar, bringing all of us into God's holy presence. The procession, which is the first liturgical act of the Mass, is symbolic of the wise men's final approach to Emmanuel in the manger at the end of their arduous journey.[18] The Magi entered the "sanctuary" of the cave, the holy of holies of the Incarnate Lord. Likewise, the bride of the Song of Songs enters the chambers, the inner room or sanctuary of her Bridegroom.

Let Us Make Haste

Already drawn by the Bridegroom, the bride makes haste to join him. When Mary heard of the sign that was given her—that her cousin Elizabeth was now expecting a child—she arose and made haste to see her and to celebrate her pregnancy (cf. Lk 1:39-56). She went in haste because she was eager to encourage her cousin, and to share her own story, to share Jesus. She walked with resolve in doing God's will in serving Elizabeth. As we travel to Mass we have the same

[18] See Peter John Cameron, O.P., Homily on the Solemnity of the Epiphany, January, 2024. Aleteia. Online at https://aleteia.org/2024/01/05/manifesting-the-whole-meaning-of-our-lives-video/

sense of purpose, eager for what we will find, and desiring to share our experience of the gospel with others. Imagine the sharing and celebration of God in their life experiences by Mary and Elizabeth while they broke bread together. That is what we do in the holy Eucharist. We come to intermingle our lives and experience the Lord together as we break the bread of the Lord's supper. Like the bride, we come in haste, eagerness and purpose.

Typically, during the entrance hymn, the priest and altar servers approach the altar in procession, bowing and kissing it as a symbol of reverence. If incense is present, they reverence it. Pope Francis explains that the altar is the figure of Christ:

> When we look at the altar, we are looking exactly at Christ. The altar is Christ. These gestures, which could pass unobserved, are highly significant, because they express from the very beginning that the Mass is an encounter of love with Christ, who, by offering his body on the cross, became "the priest, the altar and the lamb" (cf. Preface V of Easter). The altar, in fact, as a symbol of Christ, is the center of the thanksgiving that is accomplished through the Eucharist and the whole community [gathers] around the altar, which is Christ, not to look at each other,

but to look at Christ, because Christ is at the center of the community; he is not distant from it. [19]

The Sign of the Cross and Greeting

At the end of World War II, there were perhaps twenty German soldiers in a neighboring village that was being shelled by American fire in the German town of Siegburg in April 1945. The locals were always vulnerable to gunfire from both sides. On April 12, in the evening, the German soldiers were convinced to stop firing by the locals. The town priest informed the commander that the German soldiers had left and that the civilian populace had no intention of resisting any longer by bringing a white flag to the American station. All the houses were instructed to fly white flags.

The town's residents were primarily concerned about how the Americans would treat them. They had been told horrifying stories about the brutality of the Russians. What actions would these conquerors take? The Americans started scouring the area for German personnel and weaponry. There were two armed troops that arrived at a certain three-

---

[19] Pope Francis, General Audience, *Mass Begins with the Sign of the Cross. L'Osservatore Romano*, Weekly Edition in English, 22-29 December 2017. Online at https://www.vatican.va/content/francesco/en/audiences/2017/documents/papa-francesco_20171220_udienza-generale.html

room house. They paused in front of the family altar, which was carved by hand, in the living room. They entered the bedroom and discovered a stunning crucifix there. The soldiers observed the cross. They paused, removed their steel helmets, switched from right to left hand operation, and made the sign of the cross with deference. The residents of that home were no longer afraid because they knew the soldiers were authentically Christian. [20]

Indeed, the cross represents the salute of the genuine disciple of Christ, regardless of nationality, and whether one is the conqueror or the conquered. It is the Christian countersign. Among the sacramentals, the sign of the cross is among the most significant and often utilized. It is the sacred sign traced by the failing fingers of the dying Catholic; it is the sacred sign first taught to the weak fingers of the child at its mother's knee. From conception to death, the Catholic is constantly reminded of the holy sign and ceremony that represents the origin of all spiritual blessings.

The early Christian apologist Tertullian declared: "In all our travels and movements, in all our coming in and going out, in putting on our shoes, at the bath, at the table, in lighting our candles, in lying down, in sitting down, whatever employment occupies us, we mark our forehead with the sign of

---

[20] See Msgr. Arthur Tonne, *Talks on the Sacramentals* (Emporia, KS: Didde Printing Company, 1950), 63.

the cross."[21] In addition to her virtues, beauty, and attire, Tertullian most highly valued his wife's habit of making the Cross over her body and over her bed before going to sleep.[22] The Church as bride traces the cross on her body as a sign that she belongs to the Lord, who formed her from his open side as he died on the cross. By the cross she is claimed for Christ.

The Sign of the Cross is a sacramental, a holy symbol established by the Church that sanctifies an occasion or event and prepares someone ready to receive grace. It alludes to the seal placed on the foreheads of the saints in heaven and recalls the blood of the lambs marked on Jewish doorposts in Egypt on the eve of Passover. Mass begins with the Sign of the Cross:

> The whole prayer moves, so to speak, within the space of the Most Holy Trinity—"In the name of the Father, of the Son, and of the Holy Spirit"—which is the space of infinite communion; it has as its beginning and end the love of the Triune God, made manifest and given to us in the Cross of Christ. In fact, his Pas-

---

[21] Tertullian, in *The Sign of the Cross,* Bryant Burroughs (July 1, 1990). Online at https://www.catholic.com/magazine/print-edition/the-sign-of-the-cross

[22] See Scott Hahn, *Signs of Life* (New York: Image Books, New York), 26.

> chal Mystery is the gift of the Trinity, and the Eucharist flows ever from his pierced Heart. When we make the sign of the Cross, therefore, we not only commemorate our Baptism, but affirm that the liturgical prayer is the encounter with God in Jesus Christ, who became flesh, died on the Cross and rose in glory for us. [23]

The Mass also begins with the greeting, "The Lord be with you," and the people respond, "And with your spirit." We begin a dialogue: "We are entering a 'symphony,' in which various tones of voice resonate, including moments of silence, in view of creating "harmony" among all the participants, which is to acknowledge that they are animated by a unique Spirit and for the same aim." [24] By the priest's greeting and the people's response, the mystery of the Church gathered together is made manifest. [25] We convey our shared faith and desire to live in harmony with the Lord and the community as a whole.

---

[23] Op. cit. Pope Francis, General Audience, *Mass Begins with the Sign of the Cross.*

[24] Ibid.

[25] See *General Instruction to the Roman Missal*, 50, *The Roman Missal* (3rd ed.) (New Jersey: Catholic Book Publishing. 2011).

- *Reflect* on your encounter with God in the entrance procession, the altar, the Sign of the Cross, and the priest's greeting. In what way do you experience awe at the revelatory event that is beginning?

- *Pray* with Mt 2:1-12, the Magi's anticipation and journey toward an epiphany of grace, asking the Lord to help me anticipate the grace of the Mass.

4

Penitential Rite

I am very dark, but comely,
O daughters of Jerusalem,
like the tents of Kedar,
like the curtains of Solomon.
Do not gaze at me because I am swarthy,
because the sun has scorched me.
My mother's sons were angry with me,
they made me keeper of the vineyards;
but, my own vineyard I have not kept! (Sg 1:5-6)

A woman named Monica went on pilgrimage to Israel and was preparing for an outdoor Mass at the sacred Mount of Beatitudes. She prayed quietly to remind herself of the Lord's presence. Monica was thinking of intentions she might offer when she heard very distinctly, "Bring me your sin, your sorrow, and your human weakness." She was somewhat startled by this at first but then tears came into her eyes as she suddenly felt all her brokenness. At the same moment Monica sensed Jesus' eyes upon her gently accepting and loving her despite all her wounds and weakness. God was calling her to give him her misery so that he might pour out his mercy.

After some reflection, Monica realized that her encounters with Jesus had predominantly been with her "good" self, the self that accomplished pleasing things for God, the self that prayed well, the faithful and helpful self. Monica felt she was not humble enough to bring to the Lord all her wounds, her sins, her failings. But God was gently revealing to her his tender love and called for her to come, wounds and all. Monica did not need to be perfect for God, because she wasn't. Nowadays she remains faithful in prayer and tries to accomplish things that will delight the Lord. But it is above all in the offering of her sin and weakness at Mass that God has lavished grace upon grace, wiped her tears away, and wrapped her in the arms of his merciful love, making her feel completely safe. She now speaks of Jesus as her Great Consoler and of herself as his little lamb.

Shadows and Light

What a relief it was for Monica to let go of her need to impress God. Psychologists speak of the *persona*, that part of ourselves that we admire, the face we show to the world. It's fine to feel good about ourselves and put our best foot forward. But sometimes we overidentify with our good qualities and think we are better than we really are. We also forget that we are sinners. It's easy to put on a pretense of righteousness before God, our neighbor, and even ourselves. The Pharisees in the gospel had an exaggerated sense of their own importance. They loved titles and accolades. They kept the law perfectly in their own estimation. Their self-righteousness was on display for everyone to see. They wanted to impress God, others, and themselves with their air of rectitude. Jesus saw through their façade and called them to repentance.

There is another side of us that psychologists call the shadow. It is the part of ourselves that we don't like and often don't acknowledge. We certainly don't want others to notice it. Our shadow is made up of our faults, sins, and weaknesses. We might try to ignore it like dirt swept under the rug. But the shadow doesn't forget us. It often lives below the surface of our consciousness and emerges when we least expect it. Out of our mouth comes the unkind word and we wonder how we could have spoken it.

The most important thing is to bring the shadow into the light. To confess our sin to the Lord and others and admit it to ourselves. "The people who sat in darkness have seen a great light, and for those who sat in the region and shadow of death light has dawned" (Mt 4:16). God's light shines in our hearts and exposes any darkness. He does so gently, and we need not fear his light. In the light of his mercy, we discover that our sins don't define us. Most importantly, the Lord gives us the grace of repentance to change our hearts and minds. He offers us the power to turn away from sin and return to his embrace.

Repentance and Restoration

The bride in the Song of Songs has no fear of expressing her own sinfulness. She exclaims that she has not kept her own vineyard. She represents Israel, the overgrown vineyard that yielded rotten grapes (cf. Is 5:1-4). Israel was the unfaithful bride, the adulteress who intermarried with foreigners and worshiped their false gods. As a consequence of her infidelity, Israel was conquered and led into exile, first by the Assyrians, then the Babylonians. She was mistreated by her captors and made to do hard labor under the sun. The bride describes the anger of her oppressors and her scorched skin (cf. Sg 1:6). Nevertheless, because of her repentance and restoration to grace, she can describe herself as beautiful (cf. Sg 1:5). Sin disfigures us but does not destroy our goodness. We are wounded but not totally depraved. By God's grace and the salvation won for us in Christ Jesus, we are restored to friendship with God and made beautiful again.

The Church is not a museum of saints, but a "field hospital for sinners."[26] Just as Israel as a people repented and collectively acknowledged their sin, so we as the Church, the New Israel, together admit our sinfulness. In the Confiteor

---

[26] Pope Francis, Weekly Audience, August 23, 2019, Vatican News Website. Online at https://www.vaticannews.va/en/pope/news/2019-08/pope-francis-general-audience-church-cares-for-sick.html

prayer we confess to almighty God, and to each other as brothers and sisters, that we have grievously sinned in thought and deed, both in what we have done and what we have failed to do. It is important to collectively acknowledge our sin and guilt. We need to be redeemed not only individually, but as a people. When one person sins, it bears upon the whole family of God. We collectively experience shame and guilt when any Christian sins and beat our breasts to shake ourselves up and cooperate in God softening our hardened hearts. The community of saints and all the faithful are included in the prayer, which transcends the individual. The confessional phrase acknowledges the close-knit community that exists inside the Church. It is an act of humility and togetherness that embraces a shared spiritual experience and involves both the living community on earth and the communion of saints in heaven.

Mercy Meets Misery

Repentance opens us to the experience of God's mercy, which restores us to our status as sons and daughters of our heavenly Father in the family of the Church. We repeat three times, Lord have mercy, Christ have mercy, Lord have mercy—reminded of the Lord's mercy upon Peter for his threefold denial of Christ during his passion. Peter is restored to friendship with God in his threefold confession of his love for Jesus (cf. Jn 21:15-17). As with the bride, God's mercy restores our beauty and identifies us as children of God. According to Pope St. John Paul II:

> Mercy—as Christ has presented it in the parable of the prodigal son—has the interior form of the love that in the New Testament is called *agape*. This love is able to reach down to every prodigal son, to every human misery, and above all to every form of moral misery, to sin. When this happens, the person who is the object of mercy does not feel humiliated, but rather found again and "restored to value." The father first and foremost expresses to him his joy that he has been "found again" and that he has "returned to life." This joy indicates a good that has remained intact: even if he is a prodigal, a son does not cease to be truly his father's son; it also indicates a good that has been found again, which in the case of the prodigal son was his return to the truth about himself.[27]

Though we are sinners, we trust in God's mercy. He restores our beauty and gives us hope for eternal life. The bride knows

---

[27] St. John Paul II, *Dives in Misericordia*, 6 (Vatican City, Libreria Vaticana Editrice, 1980). Online at https://www.vatican.va/content/john-paul-ii/en/encyclicals/documents/hf_jp-ii_enc_30111980_dives-in-misericordia.html

that though the sun has burned her, her beauty has been restored (cf. Sg 1:5). Like the tax collector in the Temple we beat our breasts, saying "Lord, have mercy on me a sinner," and come away justified (cf. Lk 18:13).

- *Reflect* on how it helps you to consider yourself a loved sinner as you begin Mass, recalling the Lord's tremendous mercy. Of what significance is it that you do this collectively with the congregation?
- *Pray* with Sg 1:5-6 or Lk 7:36-50 and ponder redemption from sin and beauty restored during the Mass.

5

Gloria

Behold, you are beautiful, my love;
behold, you are beautiful;
your eyes are doves.
Behold, you are beautiful, my beloved,
truly lovely. Sg 1:15-16

The Mass continues with *The Gloria*, which offers us a glimpse into the magnificence of God. Assembled as God's faithful, we adore him. The Gloria, often known as "the angelic hymn," was first chanted at the birth of Christ on Earth by angels from heaven. The hymn's initial outpouring of adoration overflows into a string of exultant prayers directed toward the Father, to whom we offer thanks and praise. The Gloria then concentrates on Jesus, both as the victorious Christ and as the Lamb of sacrifice, and continues, pleading for the Son to show mercy and to atone for our sins.

Jesus Christ in his Incarnation reveals God's immense love for humanity and demonstrates the depth of His desire to be with us. God came into our world through Jesus, taking on our human nature and providing salvation to everyone who believes in Him. This glorious union of God and man is, in fact, what makes the Incarnation so beautiful and enables us to see the Lord's face. The Gloria is a hymn of exclamation based upon our gaze upon the face of God in Jesus Christ. We should also be aware that God first gazed upon us with his glorious face, smiling upon us in the Incarnation.

In the Song of Songs, the Bridegroom is gazing at his bride. She has ravished his heart, and he exclaims that she is beautiful (Sg 1:15). He then focuses on her eyes, describing them as doves. Her lively, charming eyes captivate him and enrapture his heart. We can imagine the way Christ looks upon his bride, the Church gathered. In the gospels, Jesus always gazed with love upon his people, forgiving them, calling them to himself, and sacrificing his life for them. As a priest looking out at my congregation I try to see with the eyes of Christ and mirror his ardent gaze upon his people. I am filled with love and admiration for them and desire only their sanctification. I am blessed and honored to assist their coming to Christ in these sacred rites. The Lord draws his people with love, grace, and magnetism in His eyes. We come to see the world and ourselves through the lens of his eyes as we are captivated by Him.

I once witnessed the wedding of a friend's daughter, Elizabeth to a young man named Mike. Throughout the ceremony Elizabeth frequently stared at Mike, occasionally catching his eyes. When they arrived at the wedding reception and dinner, Elizabeth couldn't take her eyes off Mike, and he returned her gaze. As their eyes locked, she smiled while holding her animated stare. Occasionally, they would go out and greet their family and friends at their tables, or have a dance together, always returning to their gaze. A few years later, I had the opportunity to ask the happy couple what they now experience as they look into each other's eyes? Mike began: "To put it simply, I feel the entire weight of our relationship in Elizabeth's gaze. Elizabeth's eyes are the first of her features I fell in love with. Not only are her eyes physically beautiful, but they are also a window to her personality, to her soul. When I say the weight of the relationship, I mean the sum of our thoughts, feelings and intentions mapped to the current moment, the past and the potential of our future."

Two Observers

Mike's response focused on lovers as both seeing and being seen. This mutual observation allows them to witness the depths of each other's soul, acknowledging the presence of the other with full attention and awareness. It is in these moments that they truly see each other, beyond the surface, beyond words, delving into the unspoken understanding that binds them. This is how Jesus sees into the depths of our hearts. He is the one who peers through the lattice of our souls (Sg 2:9), into the deep interiority of our thoughts, feelings, and the depths of our identity, which he affirms as beautiful.

Giving and Receiving

Eye contact is an act of giving and receiving. The lover offers the beloved his gaze, attention, and love, and in return, receives the same from her. This exchange is a dance of affection and affirmation, where giving and receiving are intertwined. Their eyes convey what their hearts feel, offering reassurance, comfort, and a sense of belonging. Jesus gives himself completely to us in the Eucharist. With his gaze he offers us his heart, his very being. He shares his divinity as he elevates us by grace to his own level so that he can befriend us. He meets us on our level in sharing our humanity and desiring to live in us as we live in him.

Leading and Following

In Mike and Elizabeth's gaze, there is also a dynamic of leading and following. Sometimes, his eyes lead, guiding her through his emotions, inviting her into his inner world. At other times, he follows her gaze, letting her lead him into her thoughts and feelings. This silent communication requires a balance of initiative and responsiveness, where both leading and following are acts of trust and respect. In his gaze, Jesus reveals to us the deep desires and feelings of his heart. He desires to set our hearts on fire with love for him and to set fire to the earth with the fire of the Holy Spirit (cf. Lk 12:49). Jesus eagerly desires to share himself with us in the Eucharist (cf. Lk 22:15).

Vulnerability and Steadfastness

Mike conveyed that lovers must be vulnerable and steadfast. They must practice vulnerability, breaking down their walls and reaching into what's sometimes uncomfortable to join with each other. However, they must remain resolute in their individual identities to offer strengths to the relationship. Making eye contact in a loving relationship can be a practice of vulnerability and steadfastness. It requires lovers to be open, let down their guards, and expose their true selves to one another. This vulnerability is met with steadfastness, the unwavering commitment to support each other. Their eyes reveal their feelings, joys, uncertainties, and strengths, creating a space where vulnerability is met with understanding and commitment with unwavering support.

Jesus is vulnerable with his sentiments and concerns and courageously reveals them to us, just as he shared his deepest desires to cast fire on the earth with his disciples. In giving them his Holy Spirit he set their hearts on fire and enabled them to share in his mission. In his earthly life he risked being misunderstood, used, maligned, rejected, and persecuted, hoping that some would still accept and love him. Love requires vulnerability. Jesus reveals to us the glory of being human in union with God and loving us to the end.

The bride in turn gazes upon her Bridegroom, repeating his very words to her, exclaiming, "Behold, you are beautiful my beloved" (Sg 1:16). She is captivated and overwhelmed by his gaze. Later in the Song she extols his beauty using imagery that implies his divinity: "My beloved is all radiant and ruddy, distinguished among ten thousand. His head is the finest gold; his locks are wavy, black as a raven. His eyes are like doves" (Sg 5:10-12). He alone can captivate her and give life to her soul. Acknowledging Christ as our very life is a crucial aspect of seeing his glory. Christ's face gives us life in the way a king's countenance gives vitality to his subjects. Our faith is founded on the revelation of the Spirit rather than on physical sight. Still, we can recall the look of Christ using our imagination.

Let us return to our loving couple. When Elizabeth looks at Mike in response, she senses he knows her better than she knows herself, and as one who anticipates her needs before she does:

> I guess that's what happens when you've known each other since you were thirteen. I look at Michael with love, but also with contentment, friendship,

playfulness, and admiration. I cannot say definitively why or how I began to gaze at Mike this way, but once I began, I could not stop. It was not something that was consciously done but was something always felt and understood deeply. As the Song of Songs says, "when I found him whom my soul loves, I held him and would not let him go" (Sg 3:4).

When I look at Mike, whether it is in the quiet of our home, date night at a brewery, across the room at some family gathering, one thought always comes to mind—with you it always feels like home—and at that thought, I can't help but to have a smile spread across my face, knowing that there is a profound comfort shared between us. I'll often catch Michael looking at me with a smirk, a glint in his eyes, his crow's feet wrinkling; I always ask him "What?" and it never fails that he replies with, "I just like looking at you," or "Just looking at my beautiful wife." Knowing that someone as handsome, kind, funny, intelligent, and compassionate as him, could reciprocate that gaze, see past my intrinsically flawed self, and still choose to spend his life with me, makes me feel so utterly alive. A zest for life and for all the beautiful possibilities that I can experience and won't have to do alone, simply because my best friend, my husband, is there to walk it all with me.

As we gaze upon Jesus while singing The Gloria, he is telling us that he made us beautiful in his image and that he wants us to grow more and more into his likeness. He forgives our sins and defects, seeing beyond them into the essence of who we are and delighting in our goodness. He has pledged to remain with us always and lead us to spend eternity with him. We will grow together with him into our full stature in his glory. These realizations fill us with zeal for life and wonder at our potential for fulfillment in Christ. We feel his life as we sing The Gloria.

Changed into His Likeness

St. Paul describes the transformation that happens when we observe God's glory and are beheld in his gaze, "And we all, with unveiled face, beholding the glory of the Lord, are being changed into his likeness from one degree of glory to another; for this comes from the Lord who is the Spirit" (2 Cor 3:18). This verse aptly expresses the capacity for transformation inherent in our relationship with God. Gazing upon his majesty progressively changes us to become more and more like him. His glory serves as a reminder of our continuous spiritual development and the role the Holy Spirit plays in our lives. Saint Gregory of Nyssa explains from God's perspective what happens when we come to Christ: "You came to me…therefore you became beautiful, changed as it were into my own image through some kind of mirror...you became beautiful as soon as you approached my light, drawing to yourself, through this very approach, a share in my beauty."[28] In singing of Christ's glory in The Gloria, we realize our own transformation in glory.

- *Reflect* on the mutual gaze of Mike and Elizabeth and its effects upon each other. How does gazing on the face of the Incarnate Lord in prayer transform you? Ponder his gaze during the Gloria at Mass.
- *Pray* with Lk 2:8-20 and the words of The Gloria from Mass, asking for the grace to be transformed by the glory of God as you behold Jesus.

---

[28] Gregory of Nyssa, *Homilies on the Song of Songs*, trans. Richard A. Morris, eds. Brian E. Daley, S.J. and John T. Fitzgerald (Atlanta: Society of Biblical Literature, 2012), Homily 4, 93.

6

Liturgy of the Word

The voice of my beloved!
Behold, he comes,
leaping upon the mountains,
bounding over the hills.
My beloved is like a gazelle,
or a young stag.
Behold, there he stands
behind our wall,
gazing in at the windows,
looking through the lattice. (Sg 2:8-9)

Anthony and Sue are two teachers on the staff of a large school. They have long been coworkers with a lot in common, including genuine dedication to their pupils. Sue and Anthony have joyfully worked together on several projects. They have developed mutual respect and trust over the years and each views the other as a friend. One evening, after they have spent some time together at a party, Anthony returns home that night feeling a little uneasy and confused about his relationship with Sue. A few days later, he makes the decision to tell her how he really feels. He greatly treasures her even beyond friendship and work, and desires more in their relationship. This disclosure surprises Sue, who takes some time to process it. She starts to realize that, despite her lack of attention to them, similar emotions have been developing inside of her. Sue and Anthony determine they are very precious to one another. They come to express their affection for each other, and both of their lives begin to change. A general, indistinct sense of trust and friendship turns into a decidedly passionate commitment and ultimately marriage. Over the course of months and years, the bond develops and grows deeper. They consider that initial declaration of love to be the most significant life-changing event. However, looking back, they realize that there was genuine love between them even before this articulation—more than they had acknowledged outright.[29]

Declaring His Love

The explicit expression of love changes everything, yet it utters what was, in some way, already present. In the Scriptures which we read at Mass, the Lord takes the initiative in revealing his heart. His words are a declaration of love, which he also demonstrates in deeds. In creating us male and female in love, he was revealing his inmost secret, that God is a communion of loving persons. He wants to draw us into his lov-

---

[29] See Dennis Edwards, *Human Experience of God* (Ramsey, NJ: Paulist Press, 1983), 55-56.

ing communion. From the beginning, the Lord declared that we were good. Human beings fell into sin and God's bride, Israel, fell into adulterous idolatry, but evil did not have the last word. God expressed his desire to redeem Israel, and eventually the whole human race. The eternal Word made man in Jesus Christ became the ultimate revelation of God as self-sacrificing lover. All of salvation history as recorded in the Sacred Scriptures is a testament to God's passionate and faithful love for us.

The bride in the Song of Songs waits in anticipation for her Bridegroom, who is bounding over the hills to come to her. She is listening attentively for his voice, and when she hears it, she is overjoyed at his coming. God first comes to us in his word spoken to us, and our faith comes through our hearing his word (cf. Rom 10:17). Mary heard the angel's message from God and conceived Jesus first in her heart through faith before conceiving him in her womb. We are all mothers and brothers of Christ when we hear his word and keep it (cf. Lk 8:21). When we hear and accept God's word, we are spiritually impregnated with the very life of God. We conceive and bear God's presence to the world.

After the opening rites, the Mass proceeds with the Liturgy of the Word, and we hear God speaking to us. Jesus Christ is the Word Incarnate. "He is present in his word, since it is he himself who speaks when the holy scriptures are read in the Church."[30] His eternal word speaks to us in all our temporal circumstances of life. "God, who spoke of old, uninterruptedly converses with the bride of his beloved Son; and the Holy Spirit, through whom the living voice of the Gospel resounds in the Church, and through her, in the world, leads unto all truth those who believe and makes the word of Christ dwell abundantly in them (see Col 3:16)."[31]

God's word is living and active, and sharper than any sword, able to penetrate our hearts, laying bare the thoughts and attitudes of our hearts (cf. Heb 4:12). God's word is powerful and accomplishes his purpose (cf. Is 55:11). God created all things through his spoken word (cf. Gn 1). His word is fruitful. As the rain falls to the earth and waters it, causing the seeds to grow, so his word brings about growth of his kingdom in our hearts (cf. Is 55:10). When the seed of God's word falls into hearts that are well disposed to hear and respond, his word bears fruit in abundance (cf. Mt 13:23).

Sometimes the word bears fruit in our conversion of heart. St. Augustine felt bound by his iniquities and cried out

---

[30] *Sacrosanctum Concilium*, 7, Vatican II (December 4, 1963).. Online at https://www.vatican.va/archive/hist_councils/ii_vatican_council/documents/vat-ii_const_19631204_sacrosanctum-concilium_en.html

[31] *Dei Verbum, Dogmatic Constitution on Divine Revelation*, 8. Vatican II (November 18, 1965). Online at https://www.vatican.va/archive/hist_councils/ii_vatican_council/documents/vat-ii_const_19651118_dei-verbum_ en.html

"How long, how long, why is there not an end to my uncleanliness." When he heard the word of God tell him to put on the Lord Jesus Christ and make no provision for the desires of the flesh (cf. Rom 13:14), he felt serenity infused into his heart and all darkness of doubt vanishing. Sometimes the word bears fruit in our following the Lord's call. As a young man, during mass, St. Anthony of the Desert heard the gospel of the Lord's invitation to the rich young man to sell all he had, give to the poor, and follow Jesus. Anthony felt the Lord address him personally, exited the church, and proceeded to distribute his three hundred acres of productive land to his fellow villagers. He then went off to seek Jesus more fervently in living an ascetical monastic life.

In the Song of Songs, the bride is similarly drawn to come away with the Lord in the springtime of new life brought about by the gospel, which bears fruit: Her beloved speaks to her: "Arise, my love, my fair one, and come away; for lo, the winter is past, the rain is over and gone. The flowers appear on the earth, the time of singing has come, and the voice of the turtledove is heard in our land. The fig tree puts forth its figs, and the vines are in blossom" (Sg 2:13).

Hearers and Doers of the Word

St. James exhorts us to "be doers of the word, and not merely hearers who deceive themselves" (Jas 1:22). Jesus spoke of the importance of putting his words into practice. He warned of those who respond by saying "Lord, Lord," but do not put his word into practice as being like a person who builds his house on sand. When the winds and rain come, the house is washed away. But the person who hears the word and puts it into practice is the one who builds a house that lasts on solid rock (cf. Mt 7:24-27). This exhortation to practice the gospel points to the importance of the homily, wherein the priest or deacon interprets the word of God and shows us how to live it by applying it to our contemporary lives.

The word of God also visits us through the preaching of the Lord's ministers. Preaching is an encounter with the Lord that should meet people's expectations and inflame their deepest desires. It is not enough to know about Jesus. People desire a real encounter with him that ignites their hearts with love. The disciples on the road to Emmaus had that encounter with Jesus. As he spoke and interpreted the Scriptures, he addressed their concerns and left their hearts burning within them (cf. Lk 24:32). Preaching must speak to these divine longings in the hearts of believers. Spiritual longings are often experienced as psychological needs that at their deepest level must be addressed spiritually. In addressing peoples' deepest longings, "the preacher has the wonderful but difficult task of joining loving hearts, the hearts of the Lord and his people."[32]

The Church as bride longs for the person (Jesus) who can fulfill her most profound desires. She seeks communion with Christ, her spouse, who manifests his presence through his word. She understands herself fully in relation to him. Jesus fills her with inspiration and vitality. His name and being is the perfection she desires. She learns true justice and what it means to be prosperous as his cherished disciple. "The bride of the incarnate Word, the Church taught by the Holy Spirit, is concerned to move ahead toward a deeper understanding of the Sacred Scriptures so that she may increasingly feed her sons with the divine words."[33]

The homily should help each member of the congregation to appropriate the words of the Scripture in their hearts and to live by them. Saint Euplus was a Sicilian Christian from the fourth century during the Roman Empire's brutal persecution of the Church. Euplus had a passionate love for the scriptures and frequently studied the gospel scrolls. The

---

[32] Pope Francis, *Evangelium Gaudium*, 143, "Evangelii Gaudium": Apostolic Exhortation on the Proclamation of the Gospel in Today's World (24 November 2013). Online at https://www.vatican.va/content/francesco/en/apost_exhortations/documents/papa-francesco_esortazione-ap_20131124_evangelii-gaudium.html

[33] *Dei Verbum*, 23.

emperor issued a new decree denouncing the Christians and ordering the destruction of all Christian scriptures. Instead of cowering, Euplus strode into the emperor's palace and gave himself up for being Christian. He was questioned and refused to compromise the truth of Jesus Christ. The governor took the holy texts away and sent Euplus to prison. After three months, Euplus was hauled out of jail and subjected to more questioning. Once more, he boldly declared his belief in Jesus Christ and declined to honor the heathen gods of Rome. When asked if he still kept the banned writings, Euplus acknowledged that he did. He had no book, of course, so they asked him to explain. Touching his hand to his heart, he replied, "They are within me." [34]

Saint Euplus' devotion to Christ was so strong that, rather than abandoning his beliefs, he endured threats, torture, and ultimately, death. God's word permeated the very fiber of St. Euplus' being. For each of us too, the word of our God must dwell in our hearts, be spoken on our lips, and be demonstrated by our actions.

➤ *Reflect* on the importance of expression of feelings to the Lord as seen in the example of Anthony and Sue. How do you experience the Lord's communication through his words to you, especially during Mass?

[34] Epriest, *Homily Illustration*. Online at https://epriest.com/

How do you express your love and feelings to the Lord in prayer?

- *Pray* with the story of St. Euplus and Mt 7:24-27, asking for the grace to allow God's word to become incarnate in your heart.

7

Profession of Faith

O my dove, in the clefts of the rock,
in the covert of the cliff,
let me see your face,
let me hear your voice,
for your voice is sweet,
and your face is comely. (Sg 2:14)
Who is this that looks forth like the dawn,
fair as the moon, bright as the sun,
terrible as an army with banners" (Sg 6:10)
Your cheeks are like halves of a pomegranate
behind your veil. (Sg 6:7)

The Profession of Faith or Creed is the response to the proclaimed word of God in the scriptures and the homily. The Creed presently recited during the Mass was promulgated at the Council of Nicaea in 325. In the early Church, baptisms were often performed in the context of Mass, after the Gospel. Back then, a basic profession of faith was made, usually as the response to questions. Our recitation of the Creed is a re-affirmation of what we professed (or someone professed on our behalf) at our baptism. The Creed expresses our fundamental baptismal identity, who we are and what we believe as sons and daughters of our heavenly Father.

In the Song of Songs, the Bridegroom desires to see the face of his beloved and to hear her voice. This desire is fulfilled in the Creed, when we present our faces, our identities to God and express our core beliefs with our voices. This is beautiful for the Lord to behold and sweet music to his ears. The Creed is certainly a statement of doctrinal beliefs, which are essential to being a Christian. It is not the formulas we believe in, but in the realities they express, which faith allows us to touch. But the statements do help us to express our faith, hand it on, celebrate it, assimilate and live it increasingly. The profession of faith is like reciting the pledge of allegiance every day in school, which reinforces patriotism, love of country, and shared values and principles, such as "one nation under God, indivisible, with liberty and justice for all." Just as a mother teaches us language to help us communicate and make sense of reality, so the Church, our mother, teaches us language of faith to help us encounter spiritual realities and understand and communicate that faith.[35]

Christ organized his Church as a visible society. Its members were called on not only to hold fast to the teaching they had received, but also to profess their beliefs. As St. Paul says:

---

[35] See *Catechism of the Catholic Church*, 171.

"Man believes with his heart and so is justified, and he confesses with his lips and so is saved" (Rom 10:10). Furthermore, the apostle Paul is not satisfied with ambiguous or imprecise statements. He requires that his disciples shall "Follow the pattern of the sound words which you have heard from me, in the faith" (2 Tm 1:13)." Finally, "He must hold firm to the sure word as taught, so that he may be able to give instruction in sound doctrine and also to confute those who contradict it." (Ti 1:9).

The Key that Opens the Door

We are grateful that our faith is accurately defined and can be understood and expressed in clear concepts. The Catholic apologist G.K. Chesterton explains how the Creed is like a key that opens the door to the reality of God. A key is an object with a unique and singular shape. It is something whose very existence depends on maintaining its form. Above all, the Christian religion is the philosophy of shapes and the opposition to shapelessness. It is not like all that shapeless nothingness in the eastern religions of Asia. The contours of the key are essential to opening the door:

> The shape of a key is … a rather fantastic shape . . . and arbitrary . . . A key is not a matter of argument. It either fits the lock or it does not. It is useless for men

to stand disputing over it . . . or reconstructing it on pure principles of geometry or decorative art. It is senseless for a man to say he would like a simpler key; it would be far more sensible to do his best with a crowbar. And thirdly, . . . the key is necessarily a thing with a pattern . . . a rather elaborate pattern. When people complain of the religion being so . . . complicated with theology and things of the kind, they forget that the world is complicated . . . It was also full of secrets, of unexplored and unfathomable fallacies, of unconscious mental diseases, of dangers in all directions. If the faith had faced the world only with platitudes about peace and simplicity ... it would not have had the faintest effect on that luxurious and labyrinthine lunatic asylum ... There was undoubtedly much about the key that seemed complex; indeed, there was only one thing about it that was simple. It opened the door.[36]

---

[36] G.K. Chesterton, *The Everlasting Man*, Part II, Ch. IV, Grand Rapids, MI: Christian Classics Ethereal Library. Online at https://ccel.org/ccel/c/chesterton/everlasting/cache/everlasting.pdf

An Act of Entrustment

Beyond an expression of doctrine, the Creed is an act of self-entrustment to God—handing oneself over to him, turning away from sin and Satan, renouncing them. "As on the day of our Baptism, when our whole life was entrusted to the 'standard of teaching' (cf. Rom 6:17), let us embrace the Creed of our life-giving faith."[37] To faithfully profess the Creed "is to enter into communion with God, Father, Son and Holy Spirit, and also with the whole Church which transmits the faith to us and in whose midst we believe."[38] We enter into communion with God at Baptism especially, and from then on continually in our lives. St. Ambrose explained, "This Creed is the spiritual seal, our heart's meditation and an ever-present guardian; it is, unquestionably, the treasure of our soul."[39] According to Joseph Ratzinger:

> Faith is located in the act of conversion, in the turn of one's being from worship of the visible and practicable to trust in the invisible. The phrase "I believe" could here be literally translated by "I hand myself over to, I assent to." . . . Faith then is not a recitation

---

[37] *Catechism of the Catholic Church*, 197.

[38] Ibid.

[39] St. Ambrose, *Explanatio symboli ad initiandos*, I: PL 17, 1193.

> of doctrines, an acceptance of theories about things . . . it signifies an all-encompassing movement of human existence . . . an "about turn" by the whole person that from then on constantly structures one's existence.[40]

The Creed expresses our subjective act of belief in the objective truth of reality revealed by God. Those truths about the holy Trinity, their gifts of creation, salvation, and sanctification are what make the Creed sacred. Philosopher Peter Kreeft notes: "Creeds do not say merely what we believe, but what is. Creeds wake us from our dreams and prejudices into objective reality. Creeds do not confine us in little cages, as the modern world thinks; creeds free us into the outdoors, into the real world where the winds of heaven whip around our heads."[41] God and the things of God are the fundamentals of our faith. Many people today think that being spiritual means not being religious with creeds, acts of worship, and living by a moral code. Regrettably, spirituality apart from genuine religion is typically a type of self-indulgence that deviates from a genuine and lasting spirituality. In the face of such an attitude, the Church joyfully professes her faith.

---

[40] Joseph Ratzinger, *Introduction to Christianity* (San Francisco: Ignatius Press, 2010), 54-55.

[41] Peter Kreeft, *Fundamentals of the Faith* (San Francisco, Ignatius Press, 1988), 109.

When contemporary culture waters down the teaching of Christ, "the Church again braves the media, the mouth of the world, and calmly thunders the full truth about Christ."[42] We feel in our hearts the glory of the Church as bride shining forth during the Creed, "Who is this that looks forth like the dawn, fair as the moon, bright as the sun, terrible as an army with banners?" (Sg 6:10).

Spousal Fidelity and Seeds of Truth

Echoing St. Paul, St. Ignatius of Loyola describes the Church as the devoted "true spouse" of Christ and the "holy mother" of the offspring she bears.[43] As a devoted wife, the bride of the Song of Songs wants to communicate her husband's truth and vision. She asks him to teach her because she wants to learn more about love and knowledge (cf. Sg 8:2).[44] To become more like Him in truth and love, we look to Jesus Christ for additional light from above. The phrase "spiced wine to drink" (Sg 8:2) refers to the bride's intoxicat-

---

[42] Ibid, 110.

[43] See Gregory Cleveland, OMV, *Awakening Love, An Ignatian Retreat with the Song of Songs* (St. Louis: En Route Books and Media, 2025), 330-331.

[44] The footnote for this verse in the RSVCE Bible states that many manuscripts add "she [you] will teach me," which could be interpreted as either the bridegroom (Christ) or the mother (Church) instructing the bride.

ing and enlightening experience with the Spirit, which is the wine of the Lord. As the bride of Christ, the Church puts on the heart and mind of Christ by imbibing her husband's teachings.

As the fruit of her own conversion, the bride gives her lover "the juice of her pomegranates" (Sg 8:2), signifying the Church's capacity to now share her faith in her Lord. According to St. John of the Cross, pomegranates represent the many mysteries and judgments of God's wisdom, as well as the virtues and characteristics revealed by understanding these many mysteries and judgments: "Just as pomegranates have many little seeds, formed and sustained within the circular shell, so each of the attributes, mysteries, judgments and virtues of God, like a round shell of power and mystery, holds and sustains a multitude of marvelous decrees and wondrous effects."[45] The Catholic faith's many tenets are like the bride's pomegranate seeds—they are full of strength, sweetness, truth, and the capacity to uplift the faithful. After learning from Christ, her spouse, the Church now returns the fruit of her teachings to Him by sharing her message with all peoples and globally expanding the body of Christ.

---

[45] St. John of the Cross, *The Spiritual Canticle*, Stanza 37, 7, in *The Collected Works of St. John of the Cross*, trans. Kieran Kavenaugh and Otilio Rodriguez (Washington D.C., Institute for Carmelite Studies, 1991), 617.

- *Reflect* on the Creed as an act of entrustment to the Holy Trinity. How do you hand yourself over to the Lord in surrender to his truth and love. In what ways does recitation of the Creed instill in you a sense of the glory of the bride of Christ?

- *Pray* with G. K. Chesterton's image of the key that opens the lock and 2 Timothy 1:13; 4:1-8 and ask for the grace to proclaim the truth "in season and out of season."

8

Prayers of the Faithful

And another angel came and stood at the altar with a golden censor; and he was given much incense to mingle with the prayers of all the saints upon the golden altar before the throne; and the smoke of the incense rose with the prayers of the saints from the hand of the angel before God. (Rv 8:3-4)

How sweet is your love, my sister, my bride!
how much better is your love than wine,
and the fragrance of your oils than any spice!
Your lips distil nectar, my bride;
honey and milk are under your tongue;
the scent of your garments is like the scent of Lebanon.
A garden locked is my sister, my bride,
a garden locked, a fountain sealed.
Your shoots are an orchard of pomegranates
with all choicest fruits,
henna with nard,
nard and saffron, calamus and cinnamon,
with all trees of frankincense,
myrrh and aloes,
with all chief spices—

a garden fountain, a well of living water,
and flowing streams from Lebanon. (Sg 4:10-15)

Dr. Helen Roseveare, a missionary to Zaire, told the story of a mother at their mission station who died after giving birth to a premature baby. Helen and her team tried to improvise an incubator to keep the infant alive, but the only hot water bottle they had was beyond repair. So, they asked the children to pray for the baby and for her sister. A ten-year-old girl named Ruth spoke up during the prayers of the faithful at mass, "Dear God, please send a hot water bottle today. Tomorrow will be too late because by then the baby will be dead. And dear Lord, send a doll for the sister so she won't feel so lonely." That afternoon a large package arrived from England. The children watched eagerly as Helen opened it. Much to their surprise, under some clothing was a hot water bottle! Immediately Ruth who had prayed so earnestly started to dig deeper, exclaiming, "If God sent the bottle, he must've sent the doll!" Ruth was right! Helen reflected: "Our heavenly Father knew in advance of that child's sincere requests, and he led a faraway ladies' group to include both of those specific articles."[46]

---

[46] Helen Roseveare, "The Hot Water Bottle - A True Story," Missionary to Africa | Women of Christianity, December 5, 2018.

Asking with Faith

Little Ruth's prayer was pleasing to God, particularly because she asked with faith (cf. Jas 1:5-7) that God would answer her prayer. In the book of Revelation, an angel is given a large amount of incense to mix with the saints' prayers on the golden altar in front of the throne, and the smoke of the incense rises before God, accompanied by the saints' petitions (cf. Rv 8:3). The delightful aroma of these prayers of the faithful suggests that they are very pleasing to God. Throughout the Song of Songs, the bride's fragrance entices the Bridegroom (cf. Sg 4:10-11). God is never so pleased as when we ask him for things, for he is a generous giver. In our petitioning, we should ask for the weightier gifts that the Lord desires to bestow on us. St. Augustine once commented that people ask many things of God, but few ask for God himself. His presence is better than life itself, so we should always ask to remain in his grace. We should ask for the most important gifts of salvation and sanctification, for ourselves and for others. Venerable Bruno Lanteri, OMV emphasized:

> It is better to pray according to the rule and the end that Jesus proposes, he only prayed for us as Savior, and his mission was only for our eternal salvation; for this only he labored, suffered, merited, for this only he rendered efficacious our prayer, therefore let us

> pray for salvation, and our prayer will have the same efficacy as the Lord's; if we pray apart from him, it will be useless, for we are nothing—and can't merit anything.

During the Prayers of the Faithful at Mass, the assembly responds to the word of God they have accepted in faith with intercessory prayer. They perform their priestly duty as baptized members of the Church by praying to God for the salvation of all. The congregation prays for the holy Church, for those in positions of authority over us, for people who are burdened with different needs, for all of mankind, for global salvation, and for many other specific needs. St. Paul insists:

> "First of all, then, I urge that supplications, prayers, intercessions, and thanksgivings be made for all men, for kings and all who are in high positions, that we may lead a quiet and peaceable life, godly and respectful in every way. This is good, and it is acceptable in the sight of God our Savior, who desires all men to be saved and to come to the knowledge of the truth. For there is one God, and there is one mediator between God and men, the man Christ Jesus, who gave himself as a ransom for all. (1 Tm 2:1-7)

The Church prays not only for her own needs but looks out to the world to bring its many wants before the Lord. Usually, the minister allows time to offer our private petitions to the Lord, either vocally or within the silence of our hearts. We should think about who and what we want to pray for when we come to holy Mass.

Ask and You Shall Receive

Because God is a generous giver, so we should ask him for things of great spiritual value. The story is told that one day a beggar by the roadside asked for alms from Alexander the Great as he passed by. The man was poor and wretched and had no claim upon the ruler, no right even to lift a solicitous hand. Yet the Emperor gave him a bag of several gold coins. A courtier was astonished at his generosity and commented, "Sir, copper coins would adequately meet a beggar's need. Why give him gold?" Alexander responded in royal fashion, "Copper coins would suit the beggar's need, but gold coins suit Alexander's giving."

We frequently ask God in prayer for one thing, yet he wants to give us so much more. God occasionally answers "no" or "not yet" when we ask for this "more" that he wishes to offer us. For instance, if a woman does not receive the physical healing she has prayed for, she might instead receive spiritual strength to bear her suffering and so grow in virtue, holiness, and dependence on God. We must be willing to accept God's "no" or "later" response to our prayers, keeping in mind that there is always a much greater yes. Sometimes when God doesn't grant a specific petition, he gives us something much greater in return. We should never doubt that God will give us what is best for us. He is always pleased with our asking in faith and in Jesus' name. An anonymous Confederate soldier once wrote:

> I asked God for strength that I might achieve … I was made weak that I might learn humbly to obey.
> I asked for health that I might do great things; I was given infirmity that I might do better things.
> I asked for riches that I might be happy; I was given poverty that I might be wise.
> I asked for power that I might have the praise of men; I was given weakness that I might feel the need of God.
> I asked for all things that I might enjoy life; I was given life that I might enjoy all things.
> I got nothing that I asked for, but everything that I had hoped for.
> Almost despite myself, my unspoken prayers were answered.
> I am among all men, most richly blessed!

While God sometimes gives us something different from what we asked, he frequently grants us our heart's desire in accordance with his will. A woman once kept track of her daily prayer requests, writing them in her journal. At the end of the month, she decided to look back and see how many of the requests God answered. When she tallied them up, she was surprised at how the Lord answered so many of these prayer intentions and she expressed her gratitude to God. We too ought to remember to give thanks for all the Lord has granted us in prayer.

- Reflect on God's generosity and his desire to give us the greater things in life, the gifts of his presence, his salvation, and his sanctification. Consider what you want to ask from God during the next mass you attend.
- Pray with Wisdom 9:1-18 and the story of Alexander the Great and ask for the gift of wisdom in discerning what is best for your eternal salvation and sanctification.

9

Sanctus

What is that coming up from the wilderness,
    like a column of smoke,
perfumed with myrrh and frankincense,
    with all the fragrant powders of the merchant?
King Solomon made himself a palanquin
    from the wood of Lebanon.
He made its posts of silver,
    its back of gold, its seat of purple;
    it was lovingly wrought within
    by the daughters of Jerusalem.
Go forth, O daughters of Zion,
    and behold King Solomon,
with the crown with which his mother crowned him
    on the day of his wedding,
    on the day of the gladness of his heart. (Sg 3:6, 9-11)

St. Theresa of Calcutta once said that being holy does not mean doing exceptional things. It simply entails smiling as we accept what Jesus brings our way. It means embracing and doing what God desires. We see this in the life of the first American born saint, Elizabeth Ann Seton. She came from a prestigious Episcopalian family and was a charming and refined young woman. Her parents gave her the best education possible. Elizabeth developed into a superb musician, a skilled horseback rider, a proficient French speaker, an exemplar of stylish good taste, and an entertaining socialite among New York's elite. She married William Seton and had five children. William's financial situation eventually collapsed, pushing them into bankruptcy. Subsequently, her oldest son fell seriously ill but survived. After that, tuberculosis struck and killed her husband while in Italy where the couple had traveled in the hopes of improving his health, and her father passed away soon after from yellow fever.

Elizabeth spent the following few months in Italy with her late husband's business partners, where she felt drawn to Catholicism, particularly the Eucharist. She moved back to New York and became Catholic, which caused her to be shunned by her husband's family, her friends, and most of society. She was living off donations and finding it difficult to support her five children when Baltimore's bishop, John Carroll, invited her to come and pioneer a school for girls. Thus, she founded the Sisters of Charity of St. Joseph, a new religious congregation, as well as the American parochial school system. Life was still harsh in Baltimore. She suffered from severe poverty and an imprudent spiritual guide, lost two sisters-in-law and two daughters to disease, and was still publicly ridiculed by her former friends. She endured it all for the long-term welfare of her homeland and Church. Elizabeth realized Jesus was her Savior and that obeying him was all that mattered in this life, regardless of comfort or prosperity. She expressed it in this way: "What was the first rule of our dear Savior's life? You know it was to do his Father's will. Well, then, the first purpose of our daily work is to do the will of God; secondly, to do it in the manner he wills; and thirdly, to do it because it is his will."

Her Love for the Eucharist

God wills that we become holy, as he is holy (cf. 1 Thes 4:3). Often, the Lord brings this about in ways we do not expect, by bearing the cross as he did, as in the case of Elizabeth Seton. Holiness is God's work in us, a work with which we cooperate, but cannot achieve on our own. For that, God gives us the Sacraments, especially the most holy Eucharist. During Mass, we enter the Holy of Holies, God's sanctuary. Beyond being one of God's traits, such as goodness, kindness, mercy, or love, the name "holy" signifies something more. Holy is the essential nature and substance of God. God is holy. In Isaiah, the Seraphim declare that God is exceptional, deserving of adoration. Nothing resembles him; everything was made by him. God says, "I the Lord your God am holy" (Lv 19:2). He is entirely distinct from created entities and surpasses everything. There are no human words that can fully express God, the "completely other." Nobody else is holy as God is holy. The sanctity of God remains constant, unchanged from before creation to the present, and forever.

The Suffering Servant

As we transition to the Eucharistic prayer in the Mass, we pray the Sanctus, which begins with the words from Isaiah 6:3, "Holy, holy, holy" to refer to God, the Lord of Hosts. John the Evangelist tells us that Isaiah "saw his glory and spoke of him" (Jn 12:41). Jesus is lifted up and glorified in his passion, death and resurrection (cf. Jn 12:32; 13:31) According to biblical scholar Scott Hahn, Isaiah foresaw the crucifixion of Jesus in his vision of the glory of the Temple in chapter six.[47] Isaiah elaborates on his vision in chapters 52 and 53. Isaiah begins by saying, "Behold, my servant shall prosper, he shall be exalted and lifted up, and shall be very high." Ironically, Jesus' being humbled is the very reason for his being exalted. Jesus even tells us, "whoever humbles himself will be exalted" (Lk 14:11). St. John highlights Jesus' being lifted on the cross, the most humiliating form of death, as the moment of his glory. Isaiah foresaw this:

---

[47] Scott Hahn, *Holy Is His Name* (Steubenville, OH: Emmaus Road, 2022), 124.

He was despised and rejected by men;
a man of sorrows, and acquainted with grief,
and as one from whom men hide their faces
he was despised, and we esteemed him not.
Surely, he has borne our griefs
and carried our sorrows;
yet we esteemed him stricken,
smitten by God, and afflicted.
But he was wounded for our transgressions,
he was bruised for our iniquities;
upon him was the chastisement that made us whole,
and with his stripes we are healed. (Is 53:3-5)

Jesus is the "man of sorrows." Clearly, this was not the Messiah and Savior that Israel expected. But God is holy and reveals his glory in the most unexpected ways. God's ways are not our ways. After his resurrection, he explains to the disciples on the road, "Was it not necessary that the Christ should suffer these things and enter into his glory?" (Lk 24:26)

Trembling in Awe

In the presence of our thrice-holy Lord and his sacrifice on Calvary, we ought to experience a holy fear or mystical awe. Theologian Rudolph Otto calls the holiness of God the *mysterium tremendum*, or "awe inspiring mystery," the deepest and most fundamental element of all strong and sincerely felt religious emotion:

> The feeling of it may at times come sweeping like a gentle tide, pervading the mind with a tranquil mood of deepest worship. It may pass into a more set and lasting attitude of the soul, continuing, as it were, thrillingly vibrant and resonant, until at last it dies away and the soul resumes its 'profane,' not-religious mood of everyday experience.... It may become the hushed, trembling and speechless humility of the creature in the presence of that which is a mystery inexpressible and above all creatures.[48]

This kind of emotion is expressed in the hymn, *Were You There*, when, imagining ourselves present at Jesus' crucifixion we sing, "sometimes it causes me to tremble, tremble, tremble."

In the Sanctus we relive Palm Sunday, recalling Jesus' entry into Jerusalem to die for us. Palm Sunday is a theophany, a glorious manifestation of God, because Jesus is publicly revealing himself as the Messiah of Israel. The Messiah was

---

[48] Rudolph Otto, *The Idea of the Holy* (New York, Oxford University Press, 1958), 12-13.

prophesied to enter the Temple by the East gate, which Jesus does.[49] He is riding a donkey, a symbol of peace, as opposed to the horses that conquering kings rode into cities.[50] Zechariah 9:9 tells of the king's coming on the colt of a donkey so that Israel will recognize him. Jesus will be humbly victorious over sin and death through his cross. The people wave palm branches, a symbol of victory, and cry out (as we do in the Sanctus) "Blessed is he who comes in the name of the Lord," acknowledging Jesus is the Son of God.

The Sanctus prepares us to enter this moment of glory in the Eucharistic prayer when the Lord is lifted in glory (cf. Jn 12:32). He is also elevated in glory in his resurrection from the dead. The Bridegroom in the Song of Songs is lifted in glory onto a palanquin, his throne (Sg 3:9). His divinity is revealed in the theophany of the smoke rising in the wilderness (Sg 3:6). Just as God revealed himself at Mount Sinai wreathed in smoke, and in the temple in a cloud, so now his glory is revealed in his dying and rising. His throne is inlaid

---

[49] Hebrew tradition expected that the Eastern Gate will be the point of entry for the Messiah into Jerusalem. Jesus rode a donkey from Bethphage on the Mount of Olives east of Jerusalem and passed through this gate (cf. Mt 21:1–5).

[50] However, in the book of Revelation (19:11-16), Jesus is depicted returning on a white horse—a symbol of war and power—ready to judge and make war on evil. So, while the donkey represented humility and peace during His first coming, the white horse signifies his triumphant return as a victorious King.

with precious metals wrought in love (Sg 3:10), which is at the heart of the Paschal mystery.

Renewed in Holiness

The crowd also shouts "Hosanna," which means "save us." The Jewish temple liturgy included this word on the feast of Tabernacles, when the priests processed around the altar of burnt offering while carrying palm branches and shouting "Hosanna" in praise of God for his deliverance of Israel. It became a shout of joy when the gathering of worshippers picked it up over time. Even the name "Hosanna Day" was used for the seventh day of Tabernacles. In the Sanctus, we cry "Hosanna" for the Lord to save us by his blood. We ask Jesus to come and renew us once more in the New Covenant of His Body and Blood.

The Sanctus continues with the words, "heaven and earth are full of your glory." God creates us and endows us with a human soul that is sentient, intellectual, and volitional. God makes us a temple where he can more fully dwell within us because we are made in his image with the soul's attributes. Through the holy Eucharist, the Lord flows within us and permeates every aspect of our lives. By his grace received in this sacrament, every circumstance then has the potential to bring us closer to God; people, places, things, and situations are all occasions to experience his presence. We must be more receptive to God's presence and give him full reign over our lives. We tremble as we cry out "holy, holy, holy," and are made holy by the presence and sacrifice of Christ. St. Paul reminds us of our experience of God's theophany in the Eucharist:

> But you have come to Mount Zion and to the city of the living God, the heavenly Jerusalem, and to innumerable angels in festal gathering, and to the assembly of the first-born who are enrolled in heaven, and to a judge who is God of all, and to the spirits of just men made perfect, and to Jesus, the mediator of a new covenant, and to the sprinkled blood that speaks more graciously than the blood of Abel (Heb 12:22-24).

Therefore, we should be filled with a holy fear and a mystical awe at God's glory in the sacrament of the holy Eucharist.

- *Reflect* on the awesome reality of the Lord's passion, death and resurrection that is presented to us in the holy Eucharist. Consider our share in the sufferings of Christ, our share in his victory over sin and death, and the promise of eternal life with him.

- *Pray* with Hebrews 12:22-24 and ask for the grace to grow in holiness through your participation in the mystery of Christ's death and resurrection.

10

Epiclesis

Set me as a seal upon your heart,
  as a seal upon your arm;
for love is strong as death,
  jealousy is cruel as the grave.
Its flashes are flashes of fire,
  a most vehement flame.
Many waters cannot quench love,
  neither can floods drown it. (Sg 8:6-7a)

Awake, O north wind,
  and come, O south wind!
Blow upon my garden,
  let its fragrance be wafted abroad.
Let my beloved come to his garden,
  and eat its choicest fruits. (Sg 4:16)

All life in our solar system is dependent on the nuclear fusion reaction that occurs in the sun. Hydrogen atoms are compressed together by extreme pressure in the sun's core. This sets off a chain reaction that releases enormous quantities of energy as the hydrogen atoms fuse to produce helium atoms. The sun generates around 650,000 times as much energy per second as the earth uses in a year! The earth would be completely in the dark if not for the might of the sun. The world would freeze until it could no longer support life, there would be no wind or rain, and no plant life.

Eating the Sun

Author Peter Kwasniewski invites us to a thought experiment. Suppose you could eat the sun and all its radiant energy without dying? What would ensue? You would absorb the source of warmth and light into your body. All the heat and light you could ever want, or need would be inside of you. No more lightbulbs, heating costs, or winter vacations to warmer regions. Because Jesus is, in fact, the "Sun of Justice," we get the source of all heavenly warmth and light—the heat of love and the light of truth—when we consume him in the Most Blessed Sacrament. God himself, the only Son of God, who is eternally joined to the Father and the Holy Spirit, is given to us. [51] Saint Ephrem the Syrian wrote: "He called the bread his living body and he filled it with himself and his Spirit.... He who eats it with faith,

---

[51] See Peter Kwasniewski, PhD, *Eating Fire and Spirit: The Most Wondrous of All God's Gifts,* May 30, 2018, OnePeterFive Website.

eats Fire and Spirit."[52] The Eucharist is purifying, enlightening, and unitive because we receive divine fire and its effects. Just as fire burns away impurities and turns combustible matter into itself, Jesus converts us into his Body. Like the miraculous burning bush, the spiritual soul can become spiritual fire without dying since it is incorruptible. As the sun's fire spreads light, warms bodies, and stimulates growth on Earth, the Eucharist does the same for the soul.[53]

An Intense Flame

Throughout the Scriptures, the Holy Spirit himself is often present through a flame. God led his people through the pillar of fire in Exodus 14:24 and the Holy Spirit fell upon the Apostles in flames of fire at Pentecost in Acts 2:3-4. In the Song of Songs, the blazes of our divine lover are "flashes of fire, a most vehement flame" (Sg 8:6). The fire of the indwelling presence of the Holy Spirit received at Baptism and Confirmation endows us with God's divine character and shares his being and power with us. We become a part of God's family through this infusion and regeneration. We are lovingly

---

[52] St. Ephrem, *Sermo IV in Hebdomadam Sanctam*: CSCO 413/Syr. 182, 55, quoted by St. John Paul II, Encyclical Letter *Ecclesia de Eucharistia* (Vatican City, Libreria Editrice Vaticana, 2003), par. 17.

[53] See Kwasniewski, *Eating Fire and Spirit.*

chosen through adoption, espousal, and rebirth in the Spirit. God is forever and completely united with us. We can willingly embody God's greatness now that he is within us.

At the beginning of the Eucharistic prayer, "the *Epiclesis* ("invocation upon") is the intercession in which the priest begs the Father to send the Holy Spirit, the Sanctifier, so that the offerings may become the body and blood of Christ and that the faithful, by receiving them, may themselves become a living offering to God."[54] The priest's gesture in the Epiclesis consists in holding his hands, palms down, over the bread and wine, while invoking God or the Holy Spirit to come down. The Spirit brings us to communion with Jesus in the Holy Eucharist. When Jesus gave his teaching about his flesh and blood being true food and true drink, he concluded by saying "it is the spirit that gives life; the flesh is useless. The words that I have spoken to you are spirit and life" (Jn 6:63). "Only through the Holy Spirit, the giver of life, can the Eucharistic food and drink produce in us 'communion,' the salvific union with Christ crucified

[54] *Catechism of the Catholic Church,* 1105

and glorified."[55] After the Spirit was given in abundance at Pentecost, we immediately learn that the first disciples *broke bread* together in each other's homes and were of one heart and soul in charity (cf. Acts 2:46). Already the Spirit here is guiding the Church to communion with her risen Lord in and through the holy Eucharist. "Guided by the Holy Spirit, the Church from the beginning expressed and confirmed her identity through the Eucharist."[56]

Fire and Spirit

Jesus, through the sacrifice of his blood for us on the Cross, gave us his spirit (cf. Jn 19:30). According to an ancient unnamed author, "Through the Blood shed for us, we receive the Holy Spirit. The Blood and the Spirit have been linked so that by the Blood, which is part of our nature, we should be able to receive the Holy Spirit, which is beyond

---

[55] St. Pope John Paul II, *The Intrinsic Link between the Eucharist and the Gift of the Holy Spirit*, General Audience, September 13, 1989. Adoremus. Online at https://adoremus.org/2007/12/catechesis-of-his-holiness-john-paul-ii-on-the-eucharist/

[56] St. Pope John Paul II, Dominum et Vivificantem, 62 (Vatican City, Libreria Editrice Vaticana, 1986). Online at https://www.vatican.va/content/john-paul-ii/en/encyclicals/documents/hf_jp-ii_enc_18051986_dominum-et-vivificantem.html

our nature."[57] St. John speaks of the conjunction of the Spirit and the blood and water flowing from the side of Christ at his death: "There are three witnesses, the Spirit, the water, and the blood; and these three agree (1 Jn 5:8). Cardinal Raniero Cantalamessa notes that, "Blood, like its sign, wine, is somewhat similar to fire in color and heat ('fluid fire'), and fire, in its turn, recalls the Holy Spirit."[58] An early Church Father states, "We drink the chalice of joy, the living and burning Blood, signed with the heat of the Spirit."[59] St. Ephrem remarks, "I give you wine to drink in which fire and spirit are mingled."[60]

The Holy Spirit is one with Jesus in the Eucharist. The Holy Spirit "makes" the Eucharist. The Holy Spirit came upon Mary at the Annunciation and the word was made flesh. Jesus gave up his spirit, the Holy Spirit when he died on the cross. The Holy Spirit is our very communion with Christ. St. Basil notes that the Spirit creates our intimacy with God.[61] A group of young American Catholics spent a weekend in a retreat house when, one evening, in adoration

---

[57] *Paschal Homilies in the tradition of Origen, II*, 7 (SCh 36, 83).

[58] Raniero Cantalamessa, *The Eucharist, Our Sanctification* (Collegeville, MN, The Liturgical Press, 1993), 48-49.

[59] Ancient Paschal Homily 8 (Sch 27, 133 ff.)

[60] St. Ephrem the Syrian, Sermon for the Holy Week 2, 627 (CSCO 413, 41)

[61] See St. Basil the Great, *On the Holy Spirit*, XIX, 49 (PC 32, 157).

of the Lord in the Blessed Sacrament, something awesome occurred.

> Fear of the Lord welled up within us; a fearful awe kept us from looking up. He was personally present, and we feared being loved too much. We worshipped him, knowing for the first time the meaning of worship. We knew a burning experience of the terrible reality and presence of the Lord that has since caused us to understand firsthand the images of Yahweh on Mt. Sinai as it rumbles and explodes with the fire of his Being, and the experience of Isaiah 6:1-5, and the statement that our God is a consuming fire. This holy fear was somehow the same as love or evoked love as we really beheld him. He was altogether lovely and beautiful, yet we saw no visual image. It was as though the splendorous, brilliant, personal God had come into the room and filled both it and us.[62]

This was a powerful experience of the Holy Spirit in conjunction with the real presence of Jesus in the Eucharist.

---

[62] Ralph Martin, ed., *The Spirit and the Church* (New York, Paulist Press, 1976), 16.

The Wind Blows Where It Wills

Another symbol of the Holy Spirit is the wind. At Pentecost, the disciples in the upper room heard the roar of a mighty wind. Jesus spoke of the Spirit in terms of wind: "The wind blows where it wills, and you hear the sound of it, but you do not know whence it comes or whither it goes; so it is with everyone who is born of the Spirit." In the Song of Songs, the bride now calls upon the Spirit as wind: "Awake, O north wind, and come, O south wind! Blow upon my garden that its fragrance may be wafted abroad. Let my beloved come to his garden and eat its choicest fruits" (Sg 4:16). According to St. John of the Cross: "The soul means by this wind the Holy Spirit and says that it awakens love because when the divine wind breathes over it, it sets it afire, recreates it and animates it. Breathing with its divine Spirit over her flowery garden, it thus opens all the buds of virtue, discovers the perfumes of the gifts, the perfections and riches of the soul; and opening this treasure and this inner domain, it unveils all its beauty."[63]

The bride calls her garden and his garden, one and the same. All that is hers belongs to him and the more she belongs to him the more she is self-possessed. Her only desire is to surrender more completely to his loving presence. Eliz-

---

[63] St. John of the Cross, Spiritual Canticle, Stanza 27, par. 6, in *Collected Works.*

abeth of the Trinity expresses well the identification of the soul with Christ:

> I realize my weakness and beseech thee to clothe me with thyself, to identify my soul with all the movements of thine own. Immerse me in thyself, possess me wholly; substitute thyself for me, that my life may be but a radiance of thine own. Enter my soul as Adorer, as Restorer, as Savior! O Eternal Word, Utterance of my God! I long to pass my life in listening to thee, to become docile that I may learn all from thee.[64]

This continuing incarnation, as it were, is accomplished by the Holy Spirit. Elizabeth continues: "O consuming fire! Spirit of love! Descend within me and reproduce in me, as it were, an incarnation of the Word; that I may be to him another humanity wherein he renews his mystery. And thou, O Father, bend down toward thy poor little creature and overshadow her, beholding in her none other than thy beloved

---

[64] St. Elizabeth of the Trinity, *Elevation to the Most Holy Trinity, in* Jordan Auman, *Spiritual Theology*, Catholic Contemplative Life Website, April 19, 2017. Online at https://humanityfaithhopecharity.com/category/father-jordan-aumann/

Son in whom thou hast set all thy pleasure."[65] She desires that Christ be reproduced in her by the Holy Spirit's power, to become *alter Christus*, "another Christ." She offers herself as the first fruit of the Pentecost or ingathering of the harvest. In the next invocation of the Holy Spirit during the Eucharistic prayer, through the power of the Holy Spirit, whose intercession we implore, we pray that we can become sacrifices offered to the Father alongside Christ: "May he make us an everlasting gift to you,"[66] so that we become in Christ a living sacrifice of praise.

The Bridegroom comes to his garden to taste his fruits. The bride becomes the one to prepare the banquet for her beloved by becoming a beautiful and delightful fruit, offered to the divine gardener for his joy. The Holy Spirit reveals his presence in the soul of the bride. She is the garden of the Spirit in which the living water of the Spirit flows, in which the mighty and sweet wind of the Spirit blows, in which the fragrance of the Spirit's manifold gifts float.

---

[65] Elizabeth of the Trinity in M.M. Philippon, O.P., *The Spiritual Doctrine of St. Elizabeth of the Trinity* (Westminster, MD, Newman, 1947), 54

[66] *The Roman Missal* (3rd ed.), Eucharistic Prayer No. 3 (New Jersey: Catholic Book Publishing, 2011).

One Body, One Spirit in Christ

In the final Epiclesis, we beg that through the Spirit we be brought together in the unity of the Church: "May all of us who share in the body and blood of Christ be brought together in unity by the Holy Spirit;"[67] "become one body, one spirit in Christ;"[68] "and by your Holy Spirit, gather all who share this one bread and one cup into the one body of Christ."[69] Through the holy Spirit and the Eucharist, the community as one becomes ever more the body of Christ. This is the phenomenon I experience most as a priest. As I celebrate the holy Eucharist there is an increasing feeling of unity among all of us as the body of Christ. This unity is not something we can produce on our own; it can only come from the Holy Spirit. As the celebrant calls down the Spirit upon the gifts of bread and wine placed on the altar, the faithful are gathered by the Spirit into one body and made a spiritual offering pleasing to the Father.[70]

At Holy Communion, Saint Augustine exhorts the faithful to say *Amen* not only to the truth that the consecrated host is the body of Christ, but also to the truth that they too, as individuals and as a collective, are the body of Christ: "If

---

[67] Ibid., Eucharistic Prayer No. 2.

[68] Ibid., Eucharistic Prayer No. 3.

[69] Ibid., Eucharistic Prayer No. 4.

[70] See Benedict XVI, *Sacramentum Caritatis*,13.

you, therefore, are Christ's body and members, it is your own mystery that is placed on the Lord's table! It is your own mystery that you are receiving! You are saying 'Amen' to what you are: your response is a personal signature, affirming your faith. When you hear 'The body of Christ,' you reply 'Amen.' Be a member of Christ's body, then, so that your 'Amen' may ring true. Be what you see; receive what you are." [71]

- *Reflect* on the fire of the Holy Spirit called down from heaven to make the Eucharist. How does the fire of God's love burn in your soul during the holy Eucharist? How does the mighty wind of the Spirit stir your soul with gifts and virtues? In what ways do you sense greater unity with others as the Body of Christ in the Eucharist?
- *Pray* with Song 8:6-7 and Galatians 2:20. Recall the image of "eating the sun" and ask for the grace to experience the fire of the Spirit in receiving Holy Communion.

---

[71] St. Augustine, Sermon 272, *On the Feast of Pentecost*, PL, 38, 1237.

11

Eucharistic Prayer

As an apple tree among the trees of the wood,
so is my beloved among young men.
With great delight I sat in his shadow,
and his fruit was sweet to my taste,
He brought me to the banqueting house,
and his banner over me was love.
Sustain me with raisins,
refresh me with apples;
for I am sick with love.
O that his left hand were under my head,
and that his right hand embraced me! (Sg 2:3-6)

In 1987 the film *Babette's Feast,* showing the transforming power of a sacrificial meal, won the Academy Award for best foreign language film. Babette is a gourmet chef who has fled to Denmark to escape civil war in France. She seeks work as a cook for two women, the daughters of a now-deceased, austere pastor, who never allowed them to enjoy life very much. The crucifix around Babette's neck reveals that she is a "papist." The sisters can't afford to pay Babette, but Babette offers to forego any wages in return for room and board. The sisters agree, but they never allow her to cook extravagantly and give her only meager ingredients to use to cook for the destitute. Now that Babette is cooking, the poor begin to enjoy their food. After many years, Babette receives news that she has won the French lottery. She is also aware that the 100th birthday of the deceased pastor is coming, so she offers to cook a fine dinner with her winnings to honor his memory. It takes some time for her to stock the pantry for the celebration, but finally a boat comes, and an amazing wagonload of exquisite food arrives at the house. She goes to work, preparing a sumptuous meal with soup, meat, wine, champagne, and dessert.

After spending days in preparation, Babette has a waiter serve course after course of the meal to the women and members of their congregation. One of the guests, a jovial military lieutenant, is enthralled with the course of a "Pigeon in a Coffin." He tells the guests about a French female chef who was famous for inventing this meal, how she had disappeared, and how lucky they were to share this meal. Babette remains in the kitchen throughout the meal and does not join the guests. They all are delighted as they dine, remembering the old pastor. Many divisions in the congregation are healed during the banquet as they confess their transgressions and forgive one another. By the end of the meal, everyone is transformed, savoring the moment provided by this amazing chef. Afterward, they walk out into the night, where the snow falls like manna from heaven. The two sisters thank Babette profusely and ask her where she will be moving, now that she has won the lottery. She tells them that she is going nowhere because she can't afford to move. She spent all her money on the feast.

There are many subtle Eucharistic themes in the movie that pertain to the substance of the Eucharistic prayer the priest says at Mass. The most obvious is the theme of the Eucharistic banquet, the amazing meal Babette prepares. The Eucharist is a fulfillment of God's banquet prefigured by Isaiah: "On this mountain the Lord of hosts will make for all peoples a feast …" (Is 25:6). In the Song of Songs, the Bridegroom takes the bride to the banqueting house, and his banner over her is love. The Eucharist is the sacrament of love. Spiritually, nothing tastes so wonderful as God's love, and we can endlessly feast on it: "O taste and see that the Lord is good!" (Ps 34:8). The Lord's love also nourishes us beyond natural food and gives us supernatural life.

> What material food produces in our bodily life, Holy Communion wonderfully achieves in our spiritual life. Communion with the flesh of the risen Christ, a flesh "given life and giving life through the Holy Spirit," preserves, increases, and renews the life of grace received at Baptism. This growth in Christian life needs the nourishment of Eucharistic Commun-

ion, the bread for our pilgrimage until the moment of death, when it will be given to us as viaticum.[72]

The bride begs to be sustained with apples and raisins as she swoons in her bridegroom's love (Sg 2:5). She desires that he support her with his arm embracing her and his hand under his head (Sg 2:6). The Eucharist strengthens our charity, which can become diminished in daily life, much as physical sustenance replaces lost strength. Christ's self-gift reawakens our love and helps us to sever our excessive attachments to the world and cling to him.[73] Ultimately, the Eucharist is how we will be resurrected and transformed for eternity.

Sacrifice, Remembrance, Presence

Babette sacrificed all she had to provide a meal to her guests. Her generous gift of self recalls Jesus' lavish self-giving to us in the Last Supper. He gave himself totally, holding nothing back, to the point of dying for us: "This is my body, given for you. … This is my blood, poured out for you" (cf. Lk 22:19-20). His blood is a sacrifice poured out for the forgiveness of sins. The Eucharist makes present the one-time sacrifice of Jesus crucified for our everlasting redemption. Just as Babette's guests are reconciled with each other dur-

---

[72] *Catechism of the Catholic Church*, par. 1393.
[73] Ibid, 1394.

ing the meal, Jesus' sacrifice made present in the holy Eucharist reconciles us to God and to one another.

As the guests remembered the old pastor during Babette's feast, so we remember Jesus during the memorial of his sacrifice for us. Jesus told us to "do this in remembrance of me" (Lk 22:19). The Church teaches: "In the sense of Sacred Scripture the memorial is not merely the recollection of past events, but the proclamation of the mighty works wrought by God for men. In the liturgical celebration of these events, they become in a certain way present and real."[74] Every time the Jews celebrated Passover, the event was made present to them anew in a sacramental way. They "relived it" in a sense. No wonder Jesus chose to transform a Passover meal into a memorial of his body and blood, so that we could experience his redemptive death and resurrection again and again.

Babette remained hidden all throughout the meal, while she was present only through the meal she prepared. Jesus remains hidden while present to us during the holy Eucharist. "Godhead here in hiding, whom I do adore, masked by these bare shadows, shape and nothing more."[75] His presence to us cannot be perceived only by faith, and not by the senses. We believe because of the words we have heard from Jesus,

---

[74] Ibid, 1363.

[75] St. Thomas Aquinas (attr.), *Adoro te devote*; trans. Gerard Manley Hopkins.

"This is my body, … this is my blood" (Mt 26:27-28). This faith comes to us especially through the sense of hearing (cf. Rom 10:17). St. Cyril of Jerusalem exhorts us: "Do not doubt whether this is true, but rather receive the words of the Savior in faith, for since he is the truth, he cannot lie."[76] St. Thomas Aquinas expresses it eloquently:

> Seeing, touching, tasting are in thee deceived;
> How says trusty hearing? That shall be believed;
> What God's Son has told me, take for truth I do;
> Truth himself speaks truly or there's nothing true.[77]

Finally, Babette chose to remain the sisters' cook. They thought she would be leaving them after winning the lottery, but she spent all she had on the meal. The sisters lament that Babette will remain poor, to which she replies, "An artist is never poor." Jesus, giving himself to us completely, chooses to remain with us always in the Holy Eucharist as a poor servant. When Jesus ascended into heaven, the disciples thought he was leaving them for good. But Jesus, telling them to go into the world with the gospel, added "lo, I am with you always, to the close of the age" (Mt 28:20). The Eucharist is the primary mode of Christ's abiding presence to

---

[76] St. Cyril of Alexandria, *In Luc.* 22,19: PG 72, 912.

[77] Ibid.

us. In the Eucharist, he is substantially and fully present to us in his body, blood, soul and divinity.

Participation in His Sacrifice

We offer ourselves in union with Christ in his sacrifice as we receive the holy Eucharist. The Church, the bride of Christ, is frequently shown in the catacombs as a woman with her arms extended in prayer. She offers herself and makes intercession for all men through, with, and in Christ who extended his arms in supplication.[78] According to *The Catechism of the Catholic Church:*

> The Eucharist is also the sacrifice of the Church. The Church which is the Body of Christ participates in the offering of her Head. With him, she herself is offered whole and entire. She unites herself to his intercession with the Father for all men. In the Eucharist the sacrifice of Christ becomes also the sacrifice of the members of his Body. The lives of the faithful, their praise, sufferings, prayer, and work, are united with those of Christ and with his total offering and so acquire a new value. Christ's sacrifice present on the

---

[78] *Catechism of the Catholic Church*, par. 1368.

altar makes it possible for all generations of Christians to be united with his offering.[79]

In the late fifteenth century, two young friends struggling to become artists in Germany, Albrecht Durer and Franz Konigstein, sacrificed for each other. Since their funds were too meager for both to attend university, they decided that one of them should find employment and support the other until he had completed school. Then the one could sell his paintings and finance the other's education. They drew lots and Durer went to school while Konigstein went to work. Durer turned out to be a genius. After he made a good deal of money from the sale of his paintings, he returned home to keep his part of the bargain. Only then did he painfully realize the great price his friend had paid. Franz's delicate and sensitive fingers were ruined by years of rugged manual labor. Although Franz had to abandon his artistic dream, he had no regrets but rejoiced in his friend's success. One day Durer came upon Franz unexpectedly and found him kneeling with his gnarled hands intertwined in prayer, quietly interceding for the success of Durer although he himself could no longer be an artist. The artist quickly sketched the praying hands. Today's art galleries feature many of the works of the famous Albrecht Durer, but the most popular is *Praying*

[79] Ibid.

Hands. That painting has been copied millions of times the world over, telling its tender eloquent story of love, sacrifice, labor and gratitude. The Eucharist is the Lord's loving sacrifice for us, and we ought to offer ourselves in return to him with our loving sacrifice.

- *Reflect* on the themes of Babette's Feast. How through the grace-filled remembrance of Christ's sacrifice do you become aware of his real presence in the holy Eucharist? In what sense do you experience the Eucharist as a banquet and a foretaste of the wedding feast of the Lamb? (cf. Rv 19:7).
- *Pray* with Sg 2:3-6 and Is 55:1-6 and the story of Albrecht Durer and Franz Konigstein. Ask for the grace to be sustained by the Lord's strength in your weakness.

12

Our Father

I am my beloved's,
and his desire is for me. (Sg 7:10)

Jim Croce rose to fame in the early 1970s as a folk performer. Before he gained notoriety, he was a married man who was devoted to his spouse, working hard to support her. One day, his wife revealed to him that she was pregnant with their child. Jim was first taken aback by the news, but then overjoyed. His creative inspiration and zeal were so strong that during the next two weeks, he wrote about one hundred songs. Classic singles like *Operator, Don't Mess Around with Jim*, and *Bad, Bad Leroy Brown* among them. One of Croce's most touching songs is *Time in a Bottle*. He actually wrote it for his unborn child, though most people thought he wrote it for his wife. He conveyed in it his desire to capture time and save every moment so he could spend it all with his son.[80]

The lovely intentions expressed in Croce's song, his wish to spend every day with his son, tell us something about what

---

[80] See *Behind the Music: Jim Croce*, Documentary produced by Daniel Bowen, 1997.

God wants for each of us. God the Father wants to spend every minute of every day of our lives with each of us because he loves us so much. I know many parents who have so much love for their children that they would make any sacrifice for them and desire to spend as much time as possible with them. It is then that they begin to fathom the depths of God the Father's love for his children. According to the Catechism:

> When we pray to the Father, we are in communion with him and with his Son, Jesus Christ. Then we know and recognize him with an ever-new sense of wonder. The first phrase of the Our Father is a blessing of adoration before it is a supplication. For it is the glory of God that we should recognize him as "Father," the true God. We give thanks to him for having revealed his name to us, for the gift of believing in it, and for the indwelling of his Presence in us.[81]

As Christians, we are all adopted as sons and daughters of our heavenly Father. Through his indwelling Presence he can spend every minute of every day with us now in time and forever in eternity. Jesus came to reveal the Father to us. Jesus is God's son by divined nature. He is also our brother by shar-

[81] *Catechism of the Catholic Church*, 2781.

ing in our human nature. The bride of the Song of Songs desires this intimate, familial relationship with her lover, declaring that "I am my beloved's, and his desire is for me" (Sg 7:10). We belong to Jesus and to his Father. Jesus brings us into the same intimate loving relationship that he has with his Father by the grace of adoption. Jesus teaches us to pray using the same invocation of his Father's name. Jesus is elated to have each of us as his brother or sister. We are also overjoyed to belong to our loving Father in the family of God, the Church. We have this joy in our hearts as we pray the Our Father during Mass.

When we say "Our Father," we are entering into that intimacy of Jesus and his Father. We can hear God the Father calling each of us his precious son or daughter. A Detroit priest named Edward Farrell took his annual vacation in Ireland to be present for his uncle's eightieth birthday. On the actual day, the two of them rose before dawn and dressed quietly. As they walked the shores of Lake Killarney, they paused to watch the sunrise in silence, shoulder to shoulder. His uncle then spun around and hopped along the road, grinning and glowing. His nephew asked him why he was so happy? The uncle replied, "You see, me Abba is very fond of me."[82] The uncle was aware that God took great delight in his

---

[82] Brennan Manning, *Abba's Child, the Cry of the Heart for Intimate Belonging* (Colorado Springs, CO: NavPress, 2015), 64.

life and personality. He felt deeply affirmed in who he was. That is what our Father's love does for us.

As we inherit a portion of our heavenly Father's kingdom, we participate in his divine grace and undergo restoration into his glory as his adopted children. By the anointing of his Spirit, which flows from the Lord's head to the members of his body, he transforms us into *alter Christus*, "other Christs."[83] "God, indeed, who has predestined us to adoption as his sons and daughters, has conformed us to the glorious Body of Christ. So, then you who have become sharers in Christ are appropriately called "Christs."[84] "The new man, reborn and restored to his God by grace, says first of all, 'Father!' because he has now begun to be a son."[85]

According to St. Paul: "You have received the spirit of sonship. When we cry, "Abba! Father!" it is the Spirit himself bearing witness with our spirit that we are children of God, and if children, then heirs, heirs of God and fellow heirs with Christ" (Rom 8:15b-17). St. Paul, who knew the meaning of Roman legal adoption, understood what a privilege and what a huge transformation it was for the adopted party.[86] Its consequences were momentous. The adopted person's rights in

---

[83] See *Catechism of the Catholic Church*, 2782.

[84] St. Cyril of Jerusalem, Catech. myst. 3, 1: PG 33, 1088A.

[85] St. Cyprian, De Dom. orat. 9: PL 4, 525A.

[86] See Gregory Cleveland, OMV, *Beloved Lover, The Priesthood and the Song of Songs* (St. Louis, En Route, 2023), 243-244.

his old family were cancelled, and he gained all the rights as a rightful son in his new family. He received a new father in the fullest legal sense. The adopted person became the beneficiary of his father's wealth and property. Even if new sons were later born, he remained undeniably a co-heir. Legally, the old life of the adopted person was completely cancelled. His debts were rescinded, and his slate wiped clean. His past no longer determined his identity; he began a new life as a new person. Legally he was categorically the son of his new father. Finally, the adoption ceremony was performed in the presence of seven witnesses. If the adopting father died and there was an argument about inheritance rights, one of the witnesses could testify to the reality.

The lesson of the Roman adoption law applies to us. We have been delivered from our old life of sin into the new life of an adopted son or daughter. We now belong to God the Father as his complete and special possession. Our past is cancelled, and its debts are wiped out. We now have a new life with Christ and inherit the wealth of heavenly riches. We also share the life that Jesus Christ lived, inheriting his suffering, but also his new life of glory. God the Father has adopted each of us poor, lost, helpless, and debt-laden sinners. He has cancelled our debts and granted us his inheritance. "But you are a chosen race, a royal priesthood, a holy nation, God's own people. Once you were not a people, but now you are God's people; once you had not received mercy, but now you have received mercy." (1 Pt 2:9-10). The Holy Spirit himself is witness to our adoption. The Spirit witnesses with our spirit that we really are his children (cf. Rom 8:16).

A wealthy father once had a twelve-year-old son. The boy had everything he could have ever dreamed of, except for his greatest desire, a brother. A sibling would be someone with whom the boy could spend time, play, talk, and share his father's gifts. The boy's father did not promise anything; he simply listened to his boy with understanding. One day, the father unexpectedly went to an adoption agency to adopt an eleven-year-old disadvantaged boy. The two boys got along splendidly from the start, relating like brothers from birth. They were both elated beyond measure. The adoptive son now belonged to a family, and the blood son had a brother of his own. The two lads were throwing a football around outside one day. The adopted son said to his new brother, "Gee, I wish my old friend Kenny had a football like this. He really likes football, but his father can't afford to get him one." Then he shared with his new brother how wonderful a person his friend Kenny was, to which his brother explained, "Don't forget! My dad is now your dad, too! He gives me whatever I need. He wants me to communicate with him and to let him know how I feel and what I think I need. If he thinks that something isn't good for me, he tells me. And sometimes he gives me even more than I ask for. Dad wants you to do the same thing. He wants you to communicate with him. You're his son now, just as I am. He wants you to let him know how you feel and what you think you need."[87] That day the adopted son learned what it meant to have a loving father.

Just as the adopted son realized he could ask his father for what he needed, so too can we ask our Father in heaven for what we need. In the Our Father, we pray for the petitions which Jesus deems most important to us as Christians. Beyond that, we follow Jesus' command to ask and know that we will receive (cf. Lk 11:9). "Since everyone has petitions which are peculiar to his circumstances, the regular and appropriate prayer [the Lord's Prayer] is said first, as the foundation of further desires."[88] "The Our Father is a prayer; but in both the one and the other the Spirit of the Lord gives new form to our desires, those inner movements that animate our lives. Jesus teaches us this new life by his words; he teaches us to ask for it by our prayer. The rightness of our life in him will depend on the rightness of our prayer."[89]

As we contemplate the beauty of our Father, we should desire to imitate his virtues to "be perfect as your heavenly Father is perfect" (Mt 5:48). He is slow to anger and rich in mercy and steadfast love. He makes the sun shine and the

---

[87] See Monsignor Arthur Tonne, in Mark Link, *Illustrated Sunday Homilies, Year A, B, C, Series II*, Year C, Seventeenth Sunday in Ordinary Time, 92.

[88] Tertullian, De orat. 10: PL 1, 1165.

[89] *Catechism of the Catholic Church*, 2764.

rain fall on both the righteous and unrighteous, giving sinners the opportunity to repent. So, too, should we be merciful, forgiving others as we ourselves are forgiven. As the Father is lavish in his providence toward us, so we ought to be generous in our giving to others.

We are called to be children of our heavenly Father. Jesus tells us that unless we become like a child, we cannot enter the kingdom. Children are simple and direct in expressing their needs, confident their parents will provide for them. We should imitate them in our prayer "by the contemplation of God alone, and by the warmth of love, through which the soul, molded and directed to love him, speaks very familiarly to God as to its own Father with special devotion.[90] St. Augustine reminds us of invoking our Father: "At this name love is aroused in us… and the confidence of obtaining what we are about to ask. … What would he not give to his children who ask, since he has already granted them the gift of being his children?"[91]

The cognizance of God's fatherly love is the first and most basic lesson of the spiritual life, but also the final and most sublime. Saint Thérèse of Lisieux of the Child Jesus looked for an easy and straightforward path to holiness. She uses an elevator metaphor to eloquently describe her spiritual jour-

---

[90] St. John Cassian, *Coll.* 9, 18 PL 49, 788c.

[91] St. Augustine, *De serm. Dom. in monte* 2, 4, 16: PL 34, 1276.

ney. Thérèse chose to avoid climbing the steep and arduous stairway of perfection, imagining instead an elevator that would take her to Jesus. However, there was a catch: she had to remain small, admitting her helplessness and putting her faith in heavenly mercy: "Your arms, O Jesus, are the elevator that must raise me to my Father in heaven,"[92] We belong to Jesus who brings us into intimacy with his Father's love.

- Reflect on what you appreciate most about the Our Father? How do you understand each of the petitions? As you ponder the status and rights of adopted children, what difference does it make to be able to relate to God as your Father?

- Pray with Matthew 6:7-14 and St. Therese's elevator image. Ask for thc grace to abandon yourself to the Father's care.

---

[92] St. Therese of Lisieux, *The Story of a Soul* (London, Burns, Oates and Washbourne, 1912), 90.

13

Holy Communion

I come to my garden, my sister, my bride,
  I gather my myrrh with my spice,
  I eat my honeycomb with my honey,
  I drink my wine with my milk.
Eat, O friends, and drink:
  drink deeply, O lovers! (Sg 5:1)

Set me as a seal upon your heart,
  as a seal upon your arm; (Sg 8:6)

Some years ago, divers located a four-hundred-year-old sunken ship off the coast of Ireland. Among the treasures they found on the ship was a man's wedding ring. When they cleaned the ring, they noticed that etched on the wide band was a hand holding a heart and the words: "I have nothing more to give you." The etching on that ring and its inscription, "I have nothing more to give you," could have been placed at the last supper of Jesus. Jesus said as much when he took the bread, broke it, and said, "Take, this is my body" (Mk 14:22). Then taking the cup, he gave thanks, gave it to them and said "this is my blood of the covenant which is poured out for many" (Mk 14:23). Jesus was, in effect, saying,

"I have nothing more to give you." What more can a person give than his body and blood, his very life for another? Jesus then went on to lay down his life in sacrifice for us on Good Friday, fulfilling his promise to give himself completely to save us. He rose again from the dead and bestowed upon us the promise of eternal life.

The Hebrews made sacrifices to God of things that were extrinsic to themselves—cattle, sheep, and goats. At one point the Lord told them he didn't want their sacrificed animals, he wanted their hearts in love and obedience. Jesus comes, gives his very self in love and obedience, not just something external, to the Father for us in sacrifice. Jesus left us this sacrifice, telling us to do it often in memory of him. According to St. Francis de Sales, "People remember more vividly and hold dearer the signs of love shown them in death. So when they come to die, friends are accustomed to leave to the people they have loved in this life, a garment, a ring, or an inheritance, in memory of their affection. But Jesus, in leaving this world, did not leave us a garment or a ring, but his very body, blood, soul, and divinity, his entire self, keeping nothing for himself." [93]

So now Jesus is saying to us, like the etching and inscription on the ring, "I have nothing more to give you." He has

---

[93] Saint Francis de Sales, *Treatise on the Love of God,* 1, 3: 11, trans. H. L. Sidney Lear (London: Rivingtons, 1888), 191-192. https://archive.org/details/OfTheLoveOfGod/page/n192

given everything he is, laid down his very life. He gives us the sacrifice of bread and wine, which are changed into his body and blood and which feed us. It is the pledge of the covenant in his blood, the promise made by God, that we are chosen as his people. He is totally faithful to that promise, and so we should be faithful to him. At the moment of Holy Communion, we ought to give ourselves totally to God in return to his gift of self to us.

In the Eucharist, Jesus really gives us his heart, physically and spiritually. Jesus gives us the memory of all that he said and did, especially his passion, death, and resurrection. Through the Holy Spirit, his heart memory brings his being to bear upon our entire life. We no longer perceive things only through our own eyes or with our own heart, but also through the eyes and feeling of his heart. By giving us his heart, Jesus inspires us to be like him. We ought to desire to love the way Jesus loves. To do so, Jesus tells us to live in him as he lives in us. As he lives in the Father and the Father lives in him, so he wants us to abide in him. By the gift of his Spirit, we do that through Holy Communion. We have the indwelling of the Trinity in our hearts. We experience the very life of God within, and it influences our thoughts, desires and behaviors. The character of Christ affects our deepest feelings. We assimilate Christ's opinions, values, attitudes, and inclinations to virtue at a profound level. We look at people in a way that affirms their dignity. We speak with kindness. Our identity is in Christ, and it overflows into our very being. In the Song of Songs, the bride so identifies with her lover that she asks to be a seal on his arm and heart (cf. Sg 8:6).

His Consuming Love

During Holy Communion, we are never closer to Jesus, more deeply penetrated by him, changed, elevated, and drawn into his divinity than we are at that moment. All that we are is in God. *Wuthering Heights*, the classic romance by Emily Brontë, is a fine representation of this profound reality. For the heroine Catherine, "romance" is far too sentimental a term to capture the strong primordial passions that brought her and Heathcliff together to form their marriage. The only way Catherine can express her love for Heathcliff is by declaring that she identifies herself as Heathcliff, and he with her:

> If all else perished, and *he* remained, I should still continue to be; and if all else remained, and he were annihilated, the universe would turn to a mighty stranger: I should not seem a part of it. ... My love for Heathcliff resembles the eternal rocks beneath: a source of little visible delight, but necessary. I *am* Heathcliff! He's always, always in my mind: not as a

> pleasure, any more than I am always a pleasure to myself, but as my own being.[94]

In reality, such profound union is only possible in God, and it is the aspiration of the human heart to experience it. The bride experiences this consuming fire of God, "a most vehement flame" (Sg 8:6)

In Holy Communion, God consumes us in love to change us into his being. The Body of Christ is eaten by us, and a reverse transformation occurs. Instead of our assimilating Christ's body into our bodies, as we normally do with the food we eat and digest, the Eucharist transforms and "deifies" us by assimilating us into the very nature and life of God himself. Medieval mystic John Ruysbroeck asserts: "He enters the very marrow of our bones. ... He consumes us without ever satisfying this illimitable hunger and immeasurable thirst. ... He swoops upon us like a bird of prey to consume our whole life, that he may change it into his."[95] The Bridegroom enters his bride's garden to consume in a communion of love: "I come to my garden, my sister, my bride, I gather my myrrh with my spice, I eat my honeycomb

---

[94] Emily Bronte, *Wuthering Heights*, Chapter 9 (London, TC Newby, 1847).

[95] John Ruysbroeck, *Flowers of a Mystic Garden* (London: Watkins, 1912; reprinted Llanerch Publishers, 1994), 69-70.

with my honey, I drink my wine with my milk. Eat, O friends, and drink: drink deeply, O lovers! (Sg 5:1)

When we eat, we transform ordinary food into our own bodies. But the divine food of the Eucharist transforms us into the Body of Christ. St. Augustine heard the Lord saying to him in prayer: "I am the food of grown men; grow and you shall feed upon me; nor shall you change me, like the food of your flesh, into yourself, but you shall be changed into me."[96] When we consume the Body and Blood of Christ, we truly become what we eat. St. Thomas Aquinas explains that material food first digests into the one who eats it, and then, consequently, restores to him lost strength and increases his vitality. Spiritual food, on the other hand, changes the person who eats it into itself. Thus, the effect proper to this Sacrament is the conversion of a man into Christ, so that he may no longer live, but Christ lives in him; consequently, it has the double effect of restoring the spiritual strength he had lost by his sins and defects, and of increasing the strength of his virtues.[97] The Lord Jesus speaks of the gift of his life and assures us that "if any one eats of this bread, he will live forever" (Jn 6:51). This "eternal life" begins in us even now, thanks to the transformation into the risen Christ effected in

---

[96] St. Augustine, *Confessions*, Book VII, 10, 16: PL 32, 742.

[97] See St. Thomas Aquinas, *Commentary on Book IV of the Sentences*, d.12, q.2, a.11.

us by the gift of his body and blood as food and drink in the Eucharist. [98]

- Reflect on the experience of union with the Lord when you receive Holy Communion. How do you become one with him while maintaining your own identity? What does he share with you and what do you share with him during that moment?
- Pray with Lk 22:7-30 and ask for the grace of being transformed more into the Body of Christ.

---

[98] See Cleveland, *Beloved Lover*, 120-121.

14

Ambassadors for Christ

I am my beloved's,
  and his desire is for me.
Come, my beloved,
  let us go forth into the fields,
  and lodge in the villages;
let us go out early to the vineyards,
  and see whether the vines have budded,
whether the grape blossoms have opened
  and the pomegranates are in bloom.
There I will give you my love. (Sg 7:10-12)

"Hallelujah! For the Lord our God the Almighty reigns.
Let us rejoice and exult and give him the glory,
for the marriage of the Lamb has come,
and his Bride has made herself ready;
it was granted her to be clothed with fine linen, bright and pure"—
for the fine linen is the righteous deeds of the saints.
(Rv 19:6-8)

There was once a teacher who asked her fifth-grade religion class which part of the Mass was the most important. Immediately hands were raised with likely answers: the consecration, when the priest says the words "this is my body;" the Great Amen, when the priest offers the sacrifice of Jesus to the Father; Holy Communion, when we receive Jesus into our hearts. The teacher confirmed all these answers. Eventually, a student named Billy said: "When the Mass is over and the priest says, 'Go forth.'" The teacher was surprised at this answer and suspected him of being snarky. She asked Billy why he chose that moment, to which he replied: "Because we go forth to bring Jesus to the world."[99] Billy was right in one sense. While the Mass orients us to love God, when it is ended it orients us toward others, to love and serve God in human beings.

Bearing Christ to the World

Newly transformed, we go forth from the Eucharist as Christ's witnesses. The English word "Mass" comes from the Latin word *misse,* which means "sent." The word has been used since the sixth century during the conclusion of the celebration when the priest or deacon says in Latin, *Ite, missa est.* The literal translation of that phrase is, "Go, it has been sent." Saint Thomas Aquinas writes: "And from this the Mass derives its name… the deacon on festival days 'dis-

---

[99] See Mark Link, *Illustrated Sunday Homilies, Year A, B, C, Series II*, Easter, 3A, 36.

misses' the people at the end of the Mass, by saying: 'Ite, missa est,' that is, the victim [Jesus] has been sent to God through the angel, so that it may be accepted by God."[100]

Pope Benedict XVI expands on the spiritual meaning of the phrase: "In antiquity, *missa* simply meant 'dismissal.' However, in Christian usage it gradually took on a deeper meaning. The word 'dismissal' has come to imply a 'mission.' These few words succinctly express the missionary nature of the Church. The People of God might be helped to understand more clearly this essential dimension of the Church's life, taking the dismissal as a starting point."[101] Instead of seeing the words of the priest or deacon as a conclusion to the celebration, Pope Benedict saw them as a beginning. He made that abundantly clear when he developed new words for the dismissal at Mass. Pope Benedict approved the phrases, "Go and announce the Gospel of the Lord" and "Go in peace, glorifying the Lord by your life." Both dismissals focus on the missionary character of the Mass and how those in the pews are meant to go out into the world, sustained by the Eucharist they just received. Viewed in this framework, the Mass is not just a single celebration on a Sunday or weekday or feast day, but a starting point for a lifelong journey of Christian witness. The priest, in the place of Christ, sends

---

[100] *ST*, IIIa q 83, a 4, ad 9.

[101] Benedict XVI, *Sacramentum Caritatis*, 51.

forth his parishioners into the world so that they may be beacons of light, set on a hill for all to see. The Holy Spirit transforms and sanctifies us. He reawakens in the disciple the strong desire to proclaim boldly to others all that he has heard and experienced, to bring them to the same encounter with Christ. Thus, the disciple, sent forth by the Church, becomes open to a boundless mission.[102]

The Father and Son send the Spirit so that God may dwell within us and sanctify us, reproducing Christ in us. Both the Son and the Spirit are sent as apostles to bring us into their communion of life. When Jesus concludes his mission, he sends forth apostles to complete his mission, promising he will remain with them always, until the end of time. The Spirit accompanies us and helps us go before the Lord to bear fruit for the Kingdom. Now we are not merely admirers of Christ and his teaching, but true disciples.

Christianity Is Not a Spectator Sport

We should internalize Jesus' life and teaching so that it becomes part of us and transforms us. We cannot remain content to merely know what Jesus teaches and observe it externally; his teaching must penetrate our hearts. Only then will we be able to set people's hearts on fire for Christ. We

---

[102] Ibid.

could distinguish between the admirer of Jesus and the follower of Jesus, who both stand in the crowd and listen to him speak.

- The admirer of Jesus lets the words of Jesus influence his conduct. The follower of Jesus lets the words of the Lord influence his life and burn like a consuming fire in his heart.
- The admirer agrees with Jesus that the world is a sinful place. The follower grieves because of his own sinfulness and accepts God's forgiveness.
- The admirer goes home enthusiastic about Jesus' teaching. The follower invites Jesus to come to his home and have dinner with him.
- The admirer eats bread and thanks God for his food. The follower becomes bread broken for the life of the world.
- The admirer drinks wine and enjoys good friends. The follower enjoys good friendship and becomes wine poured out for his friends.
- The admirer goes out among the crowd along the way of the cross. The follower walks in Jesus' footsteps carrying the cross.
- The admirer knows he is a creature made by God, an earthen vessel, beautiful and intact, inviolable, and safe. The follower is an earthen vessel, vulnerable,

broken for others, revealing Christ within.

- The admirer has a good life but is not fully alive. The follower has the gift of an abundant life and lives it to the fullest.

Before we evangelize, we must be evangelized by putting on Christ, sharing his desires, attitudes, and values. As we become one with him in discipleship, we follow him into ministry.[103]

The bride now is the one who invites her beloved spouse to go out into the country wherever they can be of service to others (cf. Sg 7:10-12). She is of only one mind, to do what he always desires, which is to go and bear plentiful fruit so that others may partake in his abundant life. She does all this only in union with her beloved:

> Now she has entered into a synthesis of the contemplative and the active life with no separation, for she is always not only in the presence of Christ, but she is worshipping the Father and loving his entire creation as she works with Christ to this end. Before, she experienced Christ working in her, but now he works with her. She lives in a synergy, a working with him,

[103] See Cleveland, *Beloved Lover,* 388-389.

> in and for him. Everything she does is prayer. As she rests in the oneness with her beloved that no one can take away from her, she is able to move out into the world of great multiplicity and diversity and never lose the inner "grounding" in him. And yet she is able with Christ to give herself completely to the moment and the work at hand as most important in building up the body of Christ.[104]

Clothed in Righteous Deeds

The bride is prepared for her beloved at the wedding feast arrayed in the lovely garments of her good works in union with her beloved: "it was granted her to be clothed with fine linen, bright and pure"—for the fine linen is the righteous deeds of the saints" (Rv 19:8). These good deeds follow us into eternal life (cf. Rv 14:13). St. Francis de Sales explains that the Holy Spirit who dwells in us by divine charity does these works in us, for us and with us. He does them with such exquisite art that these very works, which are wholly ours, are still wholly his. Just as he produces them in us, so do we

---

[104] George Maloney, *Singers of the New Song* (Notre Dame: Ave Maria, 1985), 145.

reciprocally produce them in and through him. Just as he works them with us, we cooperate with him.[105]

The new worship of the Christian comprises and transforms every feature of life: "whether you eat or drink, or whatever you do, do everything for the glory of God" (1 Cor 10:31). Christians, not just in prayer, but in all their deeds, are called to render fitting worship to God. Benedict XVI explains:

> Here the intrinsically eucharistic nature of Christian life begins to take shape. The Eucharist, since it embraces the concrete, everyday existence of the believer, makes possible, day-by-day, the progressive transfiguration of all those called by grace to reflect the image of the Son of God (cf. Rom 8:29ff.). Here we can see the effect of the radical renewal brought by Christ in the Eucharist: the worship of God in our lives cannot be relegated to something private and individual, but by its nature it permeates every dimension of our lives.[106]

---

[105] See St. Francis de Sales, *Treatise on the Love of God*, Book 11, Ch. 2. (Grand Rapids, MI, Christian Classics Ethereal Library, 2000), www.ccel.org/ccel/desales/love.html

[106] Benedict XVI, *Sacramentum Caritatis*, 71.

The spirituality of the Eucharist demands that we do something practical for other people. The Mass pours on us an abundance of spiritual energy which is given to carry the good news to others, especially the most neglected in our communities.

The Lord renews us at his table with the bread of life, strengthening us in love and service to others. The poet Arthur LeClaire says,

> You can talk Eucharist, you can philosophize about it, you can teach about it, but most importantly, you can pray it and do it. Sometimes you laugh it, sometimes you cry it, often you sing it. Sometimes it's wild peace, then crying hurt, often humiliating, never deserved. You see Eucharist in another's eyes, give it in another's hand to hold tight, squeeze it with an embrace. You pause Eucharist in the middle of a busy day. You listen Eucharist when you have a million things to do, and a person wants to talk. You are saying, "I give you my supper, I give you my sustenance. I give you my life, I give you me, I give you Eucharist. [107]

---

[107] Arthur LeClair, CPPS, *Wonder in the Wild, A Collection of Pertinent Essays for Christian Living* (Cincinnati: St. Anthony Messenger Press, 1969).

The Eucharist is the source and summit of our spiritual lives as Christians. Experiencing Christ's presence and love in the Mass, we are moved to go forth to bring Christ to the world. The bride, prefiguring the Church, has been overwhelmed by her beloved's love at his banquet table, the "marriage feast of the Lamb" (Rv 19:9). She is clothed in fine linen, "the righteous deeds of the saints" (Rv 19:8). She surrenders herself completely to her bridegroom and is ready to bear fruit by serving him in all her deeds. She goes forth into the fields together with him to witness the budding vines and blossoming fruits, while lodging in the villages (cf. Sg 7:11-12). So too, we go forth as Christians from the Eucharist to witness to Christ in the world, discovering his presence in persons, places, things, and events. Having received the Lord in the Eucharist, we now radiate him to the world.

- Reflect on how you feel when the Mass ends and you go forth at the dismissal. How do you carry Christ to the world in your home, work, relationships, and all the events of your life? In what way do you experience the Eucharist as the source of your Christian life?
- Pray with Sg 7:11-12 or Rv 19:6-8 while considering Billy's response to his teacher and ask for the grace to bring Christ's love in the holy Eucharist to everyone you encounter.

Praying through the Mass with the Song of Songs

Choose one phrase for devotion at each stage of the Mass

Invitation and Gathering

Let us rejoice and exult and give him the glory, for the marriage of the Lamb has come, and his Bride has made herself ready. (Rv 19:7)

The Spirit and the Bride say, "Come." And let him who hears say, "Come." And let him who is thirsty come, let him who desires take the water of life without price. (Rv 22:17)

Preparing for Mass

O that he would kiss me with the kisses of his mouth! For your love is better than wine. (Sg 1:2)

Entrance procession

Draw me after you, *let us make haste.* The king has brought me into his chambers. (Sg 1:4)

Penitential Rite:

Confiteor: Do not gaze at me because I am swarthy, because the sun has scorched me. (Sg 2:5)

Kyrie Eleison: My own vineyard I have not kept! (Sg 2:6). I am very dark, but beautiful (Sg 2:5)

Vigilance: Catch us the foxes that spoil the vineyards, for our vineyards are in blossom. (Sg 2:15)

Gloria

[G] Behold, you are beautiful, my love; behold, you are beautiful; your eyes are doves.
[B] Behold, you are beautiful, my beloved, truly lovely. (Sg 1:15-16)

My beloved is all radiant and ruddy, distinguished among ten thousand. His head is the finest gold; his locks are wavy, black as a raven. His eyes are like doves… (Sg 5:10-12)

Liturgy of the Word

Readings, Psalm, and Gospel

The voice of my beloved! Behold, he comes. leaping upon the mountains, bounding over the hills. (Sg 2:8)

Homily

Tell me, you whom my soul loves, where you pasture your flock, where you make it lie down at noon; for why should I be like one who wanders beside the flocks of your companions? If you do not know, O fairest among women, follow in the tracks of the flock, and pasture your kids beside the shepherds' tents. (Sg 1: 7-8)

I would lead you and bring you into the house of my mother, and you will teach me (Sg 8:2)

Response to Word

My beloved speaks and says to me: "Arise, my love, my fair one, and come away; for lo, the winter is past, the rain is over and gone. The flowers appear on the earth, the time of singing has come, and the voice of the turtledove is heard in our land. The fig tree puts forth its figs, and the vines are in blossom." (Sg 2:10, 13)

Profession of Faith

O my dove, in the clefts of the rock, in the covert of the cliff, let me see your face, let me hear your voice, for your voice is sweet, and your face is comely. (Sg 2:14)

Glory of the Church, the bride, professing faith "Who is this that looks forth like the dawn, fair as the moon, bright as the sun, terrible as an army with banners?" (Sg 6:10)

Your cheeks are like halves of a pomegranate behind your veil. (Sg 6:7)

Prayers of the Faithful

And another angel came and stood at the altar with a golden censer; and he was given much incense to mingle with the prayers of all the saints upon the golden altar before the throne; and the smoke of the incense rose with the prayers of the saints from the hand of the angel before God. (Rev 8:3-4)

How sweet is your love, my sister, my bride! how much better is your love than wine, and the *fragrance* of your oils than any spice! ... the *scent* of your garments is like the scent of Lebanon. (Sg 4:10)

Presentation of Gifts: *gift of self and actions*

The mandrakes give forth fragrance, and over our doors are all choice fruits, new as well as old, which I have laid up for you, O my beloved. (Sg 7:13)

O my dove, in the clefts of the rock, in the covert of the cliff, let me see your face, let me hear your voice, for your voice is sweet, and your face is comely. (Sg 2:14)

Sanctus *Approaching Theophany of Paschal Mystery*

What is that coming up from the wilderness, like a column of smoke, perfumed with myrrh and frankincense, with all the fragrant powders of the merchant? King Solomon made himself a palanquin from the wood of Lebanon....it was lovingly wrought within by the daughters of Jerusalem. Go forth, O daughters of Zion, and behold King Solomon, with the crown with which his mother crowned him on the day of his wedding, on the day of the gladness of his heart. (Sg 3:6-12)

Eucharistic Prayer

Epiclesis (Invocation of the Holy Spirit, Priest's hands over offerings)

Awake, O north wind, and come, O south wind! Blow upon my garden, let its fragrance be wafted abroad. Let my beloved come to his garden and eat its choicest fruits. (Sg 4:16)

Institution Narrative

With great delight I sat in his shadow, and his fruit was sweet to my taste, He brought me to the banqueting house, and his banner over me was love. Sustain me with raisins, refresh me with apples; for I am sick with love. O that his left hand were under my head, and that his right hand embraced me! (Sg 2:3-6)

Anamnesis (Remembering: past reality of death and resurrection made present now) "Have you seen him whom my soul loves?" Scarcely had I passed them, when I found him whom my soul loves. I held him, and would not let him go until I had brought him into my mother's house, and into the chamber of her that conceived me. (Sg 3:1-4)

Beauty of bride redeemed: Behold, you are beautiful, my love, behold, you are beautiful! Your eyes are doves behind your veil. (Sg 4:1)

Communion Rite

Our Father

I am my beloved's, and his desire is for me. (Sg 7:7)

I am my beloved's and my beloved is mine; (Sg 6:2-3)

Sign of Peace

Look upon the Shu'lammite, as upon a dance before two armies? (Sg 6:13)

Agnus Dei

Hark! my beloved is knocking. "Open to me, my sister, my love, my dove, my perfect one; for my head is wet with dew, my locks with the drops of the night." (Sg 5:2)

Holy Communion

I come to my garden, my sister, my bride, I gather my myrrh with my spice, I eat my honeycomb with my honey, I drink my wine with my milk. Eat, O friends, and drink: drink deeply, O lovers! (Sg 5:1)

Set me as a seal upon your heart, as a seal upon your arm; for love is strong as death, jealousy is cruel as the grave. Its flashes are flashes of fire, a most vehement flame. Many waters cannot quench love, neither can floods drown it. (Sg 8:6)

Concluding Rite/Dismissal

My beloved has gone down to his garden, to the beds of spices, to pasture his flock in the gardens, and to gather lilies. I am my beloved's and my beloved is mine; he pastures his flock among the lilies. (Sg 6:2-3)

I am my beloved's, and his desire is for me. Come, my beloved, let us go forth into the fields and lodge in the villages; let us go out early to the vineyards, and see whether the vines have budded, whether the grape blossoms have opened and the pomegranates are in bloom. There I will give you my love. (Sg 7:10-12)

"Alleluia! For the Lord our God the Almighty reigns. Let us rejoice and exult and give him the glory, for the marriage of the Lamb has come, and his Bride has made herself ready; it was granted her to be clothed with fine linen, bright and pure"—for the fine linen is the righteous deeds of the saints. (Rv 19: 7-8)

More books by Gregory Cleveland

- *Awakening Love, An Ignatian Retreat with the Song of Songs* (St. Louis: En Route, 2017)
- *Beholding Beauty, Mary and the Song of Songs* (Boston: Pauline Media, 2020)
- *Beloved Lover, The Priesthood and the Song of Songs* (St. Louis: En Route, 2023)
- *Consuming Love, Discovering Spousal Intimacy in Receiving Holy Communion* (St. Louis: En Route, 2024)

www.ingramcontent.com/pod-product-compliance
Lightning Source LLC
LaVergne TN
LVHW040220110826
845146LV00005B/1359

* 9 7 9 8 8 8 8 7 0 5 0 5 6 *